Australian
Inspiration

Mark Bean

BRAD

Jim Fogarty

Anne Semken

Australian Inspiration

A bush garden goes to Chelsea

Cliff Green

with Jim Fogarty

Lothian
BOOKS

Thomas C. Lothian Pty Ltd
132 Albert Road, South Melbourne, 3205
www.lothian.com.au

Contacts
www.jimfogartydesign.com.au
www.semken.com.au
www.flemings.com.au

National Library of Australia
Cataloguing-in-Publication data:

Green, Cliff, 1934– .
    Australian inspiration: a bush garden goes to Chelsea.

    ISBN 0 7344 0721 1.

    1. Chelsea Flower Show. 2. Gardens – Australia – Design.
    3. Flower shows – England – Chelsea. I. Fogarty, Jim. II. Title.

712.60994

Commissioning editor Cathy Smith
Editor Steve Grimwade
Cover and text design by Andrew Cunningham, Studio Pazzo
Typeset by Studio Pazzo

Photography by Jay Watson
Photograph of Australian Inspiration team with HRH Queen Elizabeth
courtesy Troika Photos, Chelsea Flower Show
Coloured illustration of the Australian Inspiration plan
by Brent Reid and Kathy Ewart
Back cover: Silver-gilt medal won by Fleming's Nurseries
'Australian Inspiration' at Chelsea Flower Show 2004
reproduced with permission of the Royal Horticultural Society
'Home among the gum trees' by Katherine Swift on pp. 180–81,
reproduced with the kind permission of The Times © NI Syndication,
London, 22 May 2004

Printed in Australia by Griffin Press

Contents

A word from Don Burke

IT WAS LEGENDARY radio star Jack Davey who said that his life's philosophy was 'Bite off more than you can chew and chew like buggery.' I suspect that Jim Fogarty holds a similar view. The Chelsea Flower Show is a bastion of English garden supremacy and woe betide the ignorant colonial who dares to set Blundstone upon its precious soil. Jim did.

Jim Fogarty had already established himself in Australia as one of our best garden designers. His gardens combine a wonderfully inventive modern look with down-to-earth liveability. Far too many modern gardens are stunning to look at, but uncomfortable and impractical to live or entertain in. He has won gold medals at the Melbourne International Flower and Garden Show for his designs, but the Chelsea Flower Show in London is a vastly bigger challenge.

Would an Australian-style garden appeal to the British? How on earth could you get the necessary plants, materials and garden construction crew over to England? The sheer logistics of the undertaking were terifying. Jim took on the challenge and this book chronicles his endeavours.

I will not spoil the ending other than to say that I was there at Chelsea and saw his exhibit. We are enormously proud of what he achieved, but to find out more about that, you will need to read on ...

Don Burke
September 2004

Foreword

AUSTRALIAN INSPIRATION? Australian inspiration! Who would believe that we could be inspired by Australian designers, landscapers or horticulturists? We have been doing gardens for centuries here in the UK (I think I have been designing them for about a hundred years)—who could *they* possibly inspire? Well, me for a start!

I received my first Australian inspiration in the mid 1990s when I went to judge at the Melbourne International Flower and Garden Show (MIFGS), where I quickly realised that here was an Aladdin's cave of brilliant ideas, brave designs and earthy sculptures. Yes, I was inspired by the fresh and unfettered designs being produced by Australian garden designers. I also realised that, whilst they were excellent designers in the real world, most of them had no experience as show garden designers—a totally different dimension. Here in Britain we have a tradition and history in garden shows, the five principal shows being produced by the Royal Horticultural Society (RHS). Chelsea, the flagship of the RHS, was started in 1913. So I offered to bring my seminar 'Showmanship' to Melbourne, where many of the now successful show gardeners such as Jim Fogarty learnt how to make the transition from being excellent garden designers to becoming show gardeners. Having by then exhibited more than twenty show gardens at Chelsea (my first being in 1970!) I just wanted to share some of this experience with my new friends in the Australian gardening fraternity.

It worked! I saw Jim Fogarty rise from the stranglehold of winning bronze to winning gold and best in show at the MIFGS. Congratulations, Jim, you listened—but you did it using your own strength: now there's Australian inspiration!

Inspiration is two-way traffic, which is what makes it so important in our lives. Maybe I inspired Jim—and others—but they inspired me even more. After nearly forty years as a landscape designer, I saw the truly exciting and liberated designs being produced in Australia. Furthermore, in this small world of horticulture, I was meeting new and special friends from a different culture who had the same passion I did.

Whilst I was building my Chelsea show garden in 2003, I quickly realised that every move I made was being scrutinised by the Australians: Jim Fogarty, Martin Semken, Mark Bence, Wes Fleming, and Bryan Sparling. I am really thankful that I didn't tell them to go away, that I was too busy! Over that period they all became good friends of mine, the sort of friends you know you can lean on when the chips are down. In 2004 whilst the *Australian Inspiration* team was building their first show garden at Chelsea, I was building my twenty-fifth! Keep going lads—you have a long way to go to catch up.

I have not shown every year since my first garden, but started—as they did—with a silver-gilt medal (which in RHS-speak comes between gold and silver). Some exhibitors will say that the medal is unimportant—they lie! It matters as much as an Olympic medal. On my third attempt I won my first gold—I hope the *Australian Inspiration* team will return and win gold at their second attempt. Not only do they deserve it, they have the talent to beat the rest of the field.

This book is not only inspirational, it is incredibly honest. It tells the stories of how a few people, when they share their talents, can turn a dream into a reality. It takes you through the vision, the dogged determination, the joys, the pain, the stress, the laughs, the tension and the relief.

There is no greater horticultural show on earth than Chelsea—where the judges, the media and the people's expectations are high and unforgiving. In this book you travel with Jim and the lads through all of this and I think that you, like me, will be inspired.

Julian Dowle
Gloucestershire, UK
September 2004

Acknowledgements

BASED LARGELY ON interviews with the people who created the *Australian Inspiration* garden, this book owes it existence to the generosity, patience, breadth of knowledge and enthusiasm of—first and foremost—Jim Fogarty, the garden's designer, Mark Bence, who managed the project, Martin Semken, who, with his team, built it, and Wes Fleming, nurseryman and major sponsor. Without them there would have been no garden; equally, there would have been no book. As a first generation English–Australian with pride in both the land of my birth and my ancestral heritage, I felt a strong connection with this project the moment it was first mentioned. But I am no gardener, and such horticultural wisdom as this book contains comes entirely from Jim, Mark, Martin and Wes—and from my wife Judy, who is definitely the gardener in our family.

ACKNOWLEDGEMENTS

For several weeks prior to the opening of the Chelsea Flower Show, Judy and I travelled around England and Wales, refreshing our appreciation of Britain's beautiful landscapes and visiting many great gardens, large and small. Our guides and hosts during this memorable pilgrimage were my wonderful cousins Maureen and Mick Clarke of Nottingham, Julie Phillips of Winslow, Bucks, Vivian and Steve Trew of Gloucester, and Anna and Dave Allen of Mitchel Troy, Monmouth. Anne Semken, official cook and 'surrogate mother' to the team, kindly included us in her daily catering for the much more deserving real workers during our time in London.

A great deal more goes into the making of a book than the work of its author, and with that in mind I want to express my gratitude to the people who produced the book: Cathy Smith, commissioning editor at Lothian, who has supported this project from its inception; Steve Grimwade, the often unsung copy editor; and Andrew Cunningham, whose clear and elegant design you now hold in your hand. Special mention must be made of Jay Watson, the intrepid photographer whose beautiful images grace these pages.

Finally, loving thanks go to my dear wife Judy, my first and best critic, who, as usual, travelled with me all the way.

chapter one

A bush garden at Chelsea

BY EVENING ON SUNDAY, 23 May 2004, site NR32 at the Chelsea Flower Show in London had been transformed into a little piece of Australia. After two-and-a-half weeks of construction and planting, the garden was now finished; as ready as its team could make it. Now it awaited its final test: inspection by the Royal Horticultural Society's assessors and judges, and their final decision. Had it reached the international standard required by this most prestigious of all garden shows? Was it worthy of a medal: bronze, silver, silver-gilt or—glory of glories—gold? This balmy, late-spring evening marked the culmination of more than a year of dreaming, hoping and planning; it marked the end of the heartache and sheer hard work that had brought the first Australian show garden to the Chelsea Flower Show.

The dream that became *Australian Inspiration* began, appropriately enough, at another garden show, far away: the Melbourne International Flower and Garden Show, held in April 2003. *Australian Inspiration*'s forerunner, a smaller courtyard garden, scooped the awards' pool at that show. It won a gold medal, best in the show and the designer's award. Caught up in the heady excitement of such a glorious victory, four people took the momentous decision to bring a version of this garden to the show of shows—Chelsea! These four hopefuls were designer Jim Fogarty, contractors Martin Semken and Mark Bence of Semken Landscaping, and sponsor Wes Fleming of Fleming's Nurseries. Little did they know what lay ahead: how many people would need convincing they could do it; what logistical, financial, geographical and horticultural challenges they would have to overcome; and finally, the task of building and planting a complicated, sophisticated, finely wrought garden so far from their home base. The garden now awaiting final judgement was, quite literally, living proof that they had succeeded. They knew their garden was the best they could build—but how would it fare in this fiercely contested, international arena? To win any sort of glory first time at Chelsea was, as Mark Bence said, 'A huge ask.' But whatever the outcome, the true glory of their achievement lay in the fact that they were at Chelsea; their triumph lay in the beauty of this garden and its very existence.

As you approached the site from Main Avenue, in the grounds of the Royal Chelsea Hospital, you caught sight of the unmistakable appearance of a gum tree—two of them in fact. These Snow Gums (*Eucalyptus pauciflora* subsp. *niphophila*) were about four metres tall and described by the garden's designer Jim Fogarty as 'beautiful specimens. Being multi-stemmed they had good character; rather than just one trunk, and they had a twisted gnarled look to them. Beautiful bark, the foliage was stunning.' Any further doubts you may have had about this garden's origins would have been dispelled as you drew closer. There they were—the celebrated firewood stack walls—encompassing the back of the site and part of the way along the right-hand side. They were built from 30cm-long eucalypt logs of all thicknesses and conditions, and salvaged by arborist Adrian Clancy from tree surgery jobs all over Melbourne; stonemasons Mark Stammers and Brad Peeters fitted them together like a beautiful puzzle. 'They almost took on the appearance of wallpaper,' Jim Fogarty said. 'People were amazed that they were actual logs. They thought it was some sort of artificial cladding. People said that Chelsea shows, over the years, could be remembered as the year of the floods, or of this garden or that garden, but 2004 would always be remembered as the firewood year.'

As you admired the firewood stack wall, you would have also noticed what Jim calls the lounge area. 'This is central to the garden, with the open window in the firestack wall behind. From a construction point of view, the window was probably the hardest thing to build. Everybody kept checking with me that I really did want to do that window. But it was successful. It added more depth to the garden because you could see through it to the little "secret garden" behind.' The lounge area was the feature point of the sunken garden: a useable outdoor room surrounded by ochre-coloured rammed earth retaining walls topped with bluestone-coloured bull-nose capping. The lounge was furnished with a table and benches, built of jarrah, a lovely West Australian hardwood, polished until it glowed red. Jim had 'styled' these with cushions and lumbar supports with wide charcoal and off-white stripes. A square black and white lamp had been hung above the table by landscape lighting designer Glenn McGrath. Square black plates were placed on an off-white table runner on the table and several avocados were grouped on one of the plates. 'The avocados aren't an Australian fruit, but they're Australian in lifestyle.' Perhaps this last statement summed up Jim's whole approach to the garden: 'This is not an Australian native garden. It is, nevertheless, a typical Australian garden. A true blue Australian garden with an eclectic blend of plants, indigenous and exotic, brought together in an informal and relaxed way.'

Gently playing to the right of the lounge and above the sunken garden, at a corner formed by two of the rammed earth walls, was a water feature: a fountain built of black, square-cut pieces of Victorian slate, rising in eight tiers like a pyramid. A pipe ran up the centre of the fountain and the holes were calibrated so that water ran down each tier in an equal flow. The planting on this right side of the sunken garden began with a natural colour tone of greys and burgundies and the softer Australian colours. 'The first plant next to the lounge was Reedy Grass (*Phalaris arundinacea* "Feesey"), which I originally planted in the secret garden behind the firewood. It typically spreads a little, so I also planted it in front of the firewood, because that's probably how it would grow naturally, spreading through the wood and shooting up. Then we had *Convolvulus cneorum* around the front and left side of the water feature on top of the rammed earth walls. I planted some French Lavender (*Lavandula stoechas* "Papillon") and Spurge (*Euphorbia* x *matinii* "Redwing"), which has a lime-green flower. I also had some Barberry (*Berberis* x *ottawensis* "Superba") up against the firewood—it's a little taller, with burgundy foliage. Then we had more Spurge and some Silver Spurge (*Euphorbia characias* subsp. *wulfinii* "Silver Swan"), which has variegated, silvery, creamy-coloured foliage.

'Moving away from the sunken garden and past the water feature we had Straw Flower (*Helichrysum thians* "Icicles"), with silver foliage and yellow flowers. Then there was a clump of Cabbage Tree (*Cordyline australis* "Red Star") providing some burgundy foliage between the Japanese Elm (*Zelkova serrata*)—the feature tree in the back right-hand corner—and the water feature. The shrubs in the back-right corner were the Cider Gum (*Eucalyptus gunnii*), which were coppiced and planted beneath the Japanese Elm, and we then worked our way towards the front with some more Silver Spurge and Spurge. To the right-hand side of the Japanese Elm, where the firewood meets the side fence of "mini" corrugated iron and the graduated, black-painted timber posts, I planted a taller, Red Bottlebrush (*Callistemon citrinus* "Splendens"), so where the colour palette was really soft, I added a hot colour. Coming forward from that I used some orange-pink *Grevillea*. Further forward again, towards the Snow Gums at the front right, we had another Red Bottlebrush. Then we used the dwarf Kangaroo Paws (*Anigozanthos* sp.), which were reddish–orange–pinkish; then we added some more red at the front entrance. I placed a rusted steel pot in the corner, underneath the taller Red Bottlebrush, into which I planted another bottlebrush shrub. At the front of the sunken garden, next to the barbecue, we had this beautiful orange kangaroo paw, quite tall. I called that the "orange garden" because that was the dominant plant in that area, but we also planted that part with White Bottlebrush (*Callistemon* "White Anzac"). I thought they worked really well together; it was one of my favourite corners of the garden.'

As well as being a gardener, Jim Fogarty is also a musician. The finished planting scheme on the right-hand side of the garden reminded him of 'visual music'. 'You've got the drum beat of the burgundies repeating through, finishing with the Cabbage Tree at the front right-hand entrance. Then you've got the bass line of the silver and grey-blue foliage. You've got the guitar and keyboards of the lime green, and maybe the lead guitar of the red, coming through in little sprays.' Jim wanted the planting scheme to reflect a relaxed ambience in the lounge area, 'So we used larger clumps of each plant. As it came forward towards the entrance to the garden it became a little busier, a little showier. The finished result with that right flank of the garden is that it begins quite busily, with blue in the lavender and the Blue Fescue (*Festuca glauca* "Elijah Blue") grasses underneath the gum tree, then red to orange in the *Grevillea* and then the tall Red Bottlebrush. But then the palette softens to the relaxing silvers, burgundies and green colours around the quietly playing water feature. I really wanted a story to be told in the planting. It's quite difficult to plant Australian natives with exotic species, to get the combinations right. But I was really happy with the way it finally looked.'

Raised above the sunken garden to the left, is the arbour walk, stretching from the front left-hand entrance right through to the back wall and the beginning of the secret garden, framed beneath a blue-grey painted timber pergola and floored with bluestone and granite pavers. River pebbles from the Victorian High Country have been laid in a mosaic along this path, suggesting the meander of a drying Australian riverbed. This curved shape is repeated in the 'Duckboard' jarrah garden benches that provide relief in several places around the garden, and in the black-painted wooden posts that swoop across the right-hand side fence. Most of the garden is square, so Jim wanted this swash-like figure suggesting languid, relaxed movement to counter the right-angled, four-square look. These curvaceous shapes echo the influences of a dry riverbed and the natural meander of a stream; the track left by snakes as they slither through the dust; the shape of sand dunes in the desert country; and even the path of the Great Creator Serpent of Aboriginal legend.

'As you walked beneath the arbour towards the back of the garden you would notice an open screen of widely spaced, rusted reinforcing mesh, where we had honeysuckle growing up, right to the top of the arbour. Many of the tendrils reached the top, so the bulk of it was three-quarters of the way up. This formed a nice green screen on the right-hand side, separating the lounge area and the sunken garden from the arbour walk.' On the left-hand side of the arbour walk Jim had planting which was really bold. 'Julian Dowle (doyen of Chelsea designers) told me it made a statement. It was like putting down a full stop, creating a precise boundary to the garden. It was not meant to be relaxing; it had to balance up the whole garden. We had staggered plantings of the Cabbage Tree—its burgundy, spiky foliage just sticking up through balls of Box Hedge (*Buxus sempervirens*) and the lime-green, haphazard flowers of Spurge. Lavender was sprinkled around the edges, as were the Australian wildflowers: Outback Daisy (*Brachycome* sp.) and Outback Fan Flower (*Scaevola* sp). Many people were confused by these Australian wildflowers because they looked so like English daisies. Further along, on the left, was another of Matt Heritage's jarrah garden benches, curved into an elongated "S" shape, echoing the pebble mosaic. We had two rusted steel pots with Cabbage Trees in them, and Glenn McGrath placed lights right along the top of the arbour posts so the walk was illuminated at night.' The arbour walk terminated at the firewood wall, with a straight jarrah bench in front. 'We had Photinia on either side of the straight bench at the end—they're a creamy-white, hydrangea-like flower. A good thing about this garden was that there were four different seating areas—as well as the bull-nosing on the retaining walls—so it had several areas for small groups of people to gather for private conversation.'

To the right, at the end of the arbour walk, was the entrance to the secret garden, which you could see from the rear bench. This secret garden was also visible from outside the garden, from the laneway running beside the site. Little more than a mysterious passage, the secret garden was a series of rectangular paving steppers, leading to another tapering water feature at the end, similar to the fountain in the front garden, except here the sawn slate slabs were rectangular. The largest stone, the base of the pyramid, was actually the last of the steppers, measuring 80cm by 40cm. 'On the left of the secret garden was a rusted sheet steel back wall. We had an espaliered Red Bottlebrush hedge growing along this wall, which had just begun flowering. We actually planted the espaliered bottlebrushes in two rows, alternating them to give them a hedge-like appearance—a double thickness. They were opening up, these vibrant Red Bottlebrush flowers, against the rusted steel. Again, the firewood was at the end of the secret garden and I had the Reedy Grass on the right-hand side of the water feature, planting the Blue Fescue grasses between and around the steppers. The planting in the secret garden was rustic; very natural, a little overgrown and wild, a little meadow-like; not so manicured, except we clipped the grasses between the steppers into little domes. That was all the "manicuring" we did in there. We wanted to evoke a mysterious, untended, secret garden feel. On the right-hand side was the back of the firewood wall, which was rough and irregular, almost eccentric. The logs were meant to be 30cm long, but the arborist, cutting with a chainsaw, isn't going to get them all exact. They were flush at the front, almost like wallpaper, but on the back they varied by up to 8cm. There were a few that stuck out even further, but we cut those off with a handsaw.' When the sun rose diagonally across the back of the site, the oblique light hit the secret garden, creating a myriad of shadows across the logs, deepening the sense of mystery.

'From the arbour walk you can step back down into the sunken garden.' Three redgum sleepers were set into the lawn, 'angled towards the lounge area. They directed your eye towards the nucleus of the garden, which was the lounge area. Also, as you stepped down from the arbour into the sunken garden you saw the stainless steel barbecue on the right, which gave the garden a modern, sophisticated twist; also a personable touch. As soon as people saw the barbecue they could envisage themselves in this garden; it instantly became a functional garden. The barbecue is on your right when you step off the arbour walk into the sunken garden, then immediately to your left is the jarrah table and the benches with their comfortable cushions. It's a very welcoming garden.' One UK visitor remarked, 'I feel like I just want to step down into that garden, sit down at that beautiful table and enjoy a glass of Australian wine or a cold beer.'

When it was decided, quite early in the life of the project, that the garden would be named *Australian Inspiration*, we immediately knew we could not find a better title for this book. But we also knew it was not enough. The word 'garden' had to be in there somewhere, so potential readers would have some idea of what we were on about. The sub-title 'An Australian garden goes to Chelsea' came immediately to mind, except repeating the word 'Australian' seemed a bit much; jingoistic in fact; certainly not euphonious. We needed another word for 'Australian'. A 'down under' garden, perhaps, or an 'antipodean' garden? Down under what, and antipodean to where, and what century were we in, anyway? What single word conjures up an image of Australia all around the world? 'Outback', perhaps. It also suggests deserts and other arid open spaces. Wrong image. Well, it is a 'Melbourne' garden. 'A Melbourne garden goes to Chelsea' is accurate but too limiting and parochial. Why not call it a 'bush garden'? But to many Australians a 'bush garden' is an Australian native garden, with exotic plants strictly excluded, a form of botanical purity, if you like. *Australian Inspiration* was never conceived as a native Australian garden—but how 'native' is 'the bush', anyway? Apart from some fragments of rainforest, a few pristine coastal areas and the mountains and lakes of western Tasmania, much of the continent has been invaded by exotic plants. Many of our national parks have been compromised, sometimes irretrievably.

Perhaps the Australian landscape, like the Australian population, is now a great blending of the native and the exotic. Walk into the bush, almost anywhere across the continent, and you may stumble across remnants of earlier settlement: a slab hut, overgrown and decaying, perhaps a brick chimney—all that remains of a deserted farmhouse or cottage. All trace of the buildings and fences may be gone, but something always remains: the plants. Climbing roses, hawthorn bushes, swathes of jonquils and freesias, rows of blue and white *Agapanthus* lining a long-gone driveway, and always—inevitably—red geraniums. A few gnarled old apple trees may indicate where an orchard once thrived; but above all else, towering above, their fresh green canopies intermingled with the wattles and eucalypts, could be the great forest trees of Britain and Europe: elms, oaks, poplars, and willows lining streams and rivers.

Travel east from Melbourne, leave the Princes Freeway at Moe and drive deep into the Gippsland forest. Suddenly you will come upon a steep-sided valley, where 150-year-old European trees blend with the Australian bush, creating a landscape so beautiful you catch your breath. This is Walhalla, an abandoned goldmining town once thriving and prosperous, now almost deserted; surely one of the loveliest places on earth.

From the first beginnings of European settlement the white invaders struggled to recreate the gardens and natural landscapes of England, Ireland, Scotland and Wales in their adopted home. The native 'bush', originally slandered as 'colourless and scentless', was rigorously excluded: chopped down if possible, fenced out always. Public parks were beautiful oases of European trees, holding at bay the grey–green monotony of the native 'scrub'. Everyone's garden was strictly exotic, except perhaps for one lovely specimen of *Eucalyptus ficifolia,* the ubiquitous Flowering Gum. Then came the backlash. In a dry climate, European gardens require a great deal of water, and Australia is the driest continent on earth. From the end of World War II a heightened sense of nationalism crept across the land. Australian sporting prowess had always been celebrated, but it reached a peak with the Melbourne Olympics in 1956. This was followed by a heightened interest in Australian literature, theatre and, finally, movies. By the 1970s horticulture had been well and truly recruited and 'native' gardens were springing up across the suburbs of our cities and beyond. 'Dry' gardens became the overwhelming trend. Lawns were dug out and Australian trees and shrubs were planted in overwhelming profusion. Some of these gardens were well conceived, with a firm understanding of the ecology of local plant life, teamed with rocks and water to create natural-looking, peaceful landscapes. But many were haphazard and ill-considered plantings, perhaps of materials from elsewhere in Australia, much of it unsuited to its new and equally 'foreign' environment. Also, the relatively short life span of some of the native species and their vulnerability to fire were not considered, and after a few years many of these gardens became thickets of grey, tinder-dry sticks and litter crackling underfoot; caches of fuel awaiting the possibility of a disastrous bushfire. So, as with any movement that degenerates into a fad, the wheel of fashion turned again and soon 'cottage gardens' of flowering English shrubs and annuals began appearing among the wattles, eucalypts and bottlebrushes. The effect was pleasing and the marriage appears successful. This blending of influences from all around the world is perhaps a principal reason for Australia's success in the world, in horticulture no less than any other field of endeavour. *Australian Inspiration* epitomises the success of this happy blending.

The Australian 'bush' is a romantic place, a state of mind. It exists as much in our cities, towns and suburbs as it does in our countryside and outback. It is a cultural entity rather than a geographical location. It is where our stories and legends are set, where our heroes live, where our spirit dwells. It is—to both black and white Australians—our *dreaming*. So, on a balmy evening in the dying days of a London spring, as a group of young Australians put the finishing touches to their garden, they anxiously awaited judgement day, when the experienced assessors and learned judges of that august body, the Royal Horticultural Society, would come by and consider every leaf and flower, examine every mortise join and detail of construction. Then, like all the other anxious gardeners, they would wait another interminable day before discovering their fate; to see if they were to be rewarded at the end of their dreaming, to find out if they had successfully mined bronze, silver, silver-gilt or gold.

chapter two

Down the garden path

WHEN JIM FOGARTY left school in 1988 he had no idea he would become a designer of gold-medal winning gardens. His secondary schooling was one of the best money could buy. He matriculated with his Higher School Certificate from Melbourne Grammar, one of Australia's most prestigious schools. 'I was never really enthused by anything at school. Melbourne Grammar, I guess, is an institution for lawyers and doctors and accountants. It gave me no grounding for what I'm doing now. I left school, not really sure of what I was going to do.' He began a business studies course at the University of Melbourne, but left after two weeks. 'All theory and bullshit,' was how he later described those 10 wasted days: 'I guess I just wanted to get out there and do the real thing, not learn about it in a lecture room. Maybe I'm not a theoretical person. Maybe I just preferred to do it myself and learn the hard way.'

But he had his music. Jim wasn't a formally trained musician but had been playing guitar since he was 15. He had bought a guitar and a tape recorder and taught himself to play. He never learned to read music but joined a band at school; music providing an abiding interest and a steady, modest income well into those precarious years that followed school. He and his fellow band members played more than 300 gigs across nine years at venues in Melbourne and around Victoria. Jim still listens to music 'all the time' as he works, in the car and at home. 'I can hear every instrument individually.' The arrangement sounds in his head and he seems to understand how the pieces are fitting together. 'When I design gardens now I still treat it very much like a symphony of plants,' each part combining to create the entire design.

Jim's first full-time job after school was cutting firewood in a woodyard in the inner-Melbourne industrial suburb of Kensington. Twenty-six-tonne trucks would come down from the mountain forests to the woodyard, the logs would be unloaded and Jim and his workmates would split them, cut them into firewood lengths, split them again, load them onto smaller trucks and deliver them to restaurants, cafes and homes around Melbourne and the suburbs. Jim loved the work and the mateship. This time marked the beginning of his passion for hard physical labour and outdoor work in all weathers.

We don't know what Jim's parents thought of this, but we can imagine that they were not too impressed. His father, who had made a career selling medical products and equipment, rising to become managing director of an international company, had attended Melbourne Grammar, as did Jim's two brothers. His parents lived in the leafy, upper middle-class suburb of Hawthorn. His father attended to the garden; lovingly but with little knowledge and less skill: 'He'll climb up and cut off the branch he's holding onto and fall. He'll water when it's raining. He's a clumsy gardener, but he loves it. As a kid I watched him and wondered what he was doing, but to become a gardener would have been the last thing I ever imagined doing.'

Soon after leaving school Jim joined the Army Reserve. His grand-father, Tom Fogarty, had been a career soldier in the Australian army, rising to the rank of brigadier. Jim never knew him—he died when Jim's father was quite young. Jim served part-time in the infantry for two years and greatly enjoyed the experience: 'pushing yourself harder than you've ever known you could; surviving on three or four hours' sleep; living on not much food; operating mostly at night. Then there's the mateship.'

Looking back now Jim realises that his army experience gave him something that was to greatly influence his future working life: a love of the Australian bush. Jim found that in the infantry you are trained to blend into the bush, to become part of it, to somehow think like a bush creature. He became what he calls a 'bush insider' and remembers creeping to within a few metres of civilians camping in the bush without them knowing anyone was there. Above all he learned to appreciate the solitude of the bush, its muted colours, the play of sunlight on blossom, of moonlight on leaves, the ever-changing textures and colours of bark on the trunks of eucalypts, and the subtlety of changes moving with the barely perceptible flow of the seasons; all invisible to those who do not know and love the Australian bush.

The Army Reserve, playing in the band and his job at the woodyard filled Jim's life during those first few years after leaving school, but he knew he would soon have to settle down and obtain some sort of qualification. A workmate at the woodyard had enrolled at Burnley Horticultural College. This sounded interesting: outdoor work, hands in the soil, perhaps the next best thing to actually working in the bush. Jim 'checked it out' and liked what he saw. The campus is set in extensive landscaped gardens, the course covers all aspects of horticulture, including botany, soil science, garden design and construction, but with a great deal of emphasis on practical, hands-on work. You learned about it, then you did it; so different from university. Jim applied for a place but was unsuccessful: 'It was pretty competitive, and I just didn't have the marks from school. At that time landscaping was pretty trendy. Every Tom, Dick or Harry, every bloke with a ute, wanted to be a landscaper.' Jim did not accept this situation. He wangled an interview with Dr Peter May, one of the senior lecturers at the college: 'I let him know how keen I was. I'd been out of school for a few years, knocked around, but now I was ready to study.' Several weeks passed and finally Dr May rang Jim, asked if he was still keen and told him there was a place for him if he wanted it. Jim believes this was a 'third round offer', which means he was twice passed over to study for the career at which he has since excelled. Dr May now sees Jim each year at the Melbourne International Flower and Garden Show. 'You've done well,' he says, as he gives Jim a proud wink.

Jim completed his course in two years full-time, working from 8.30am to 5.30pm most weekdays, completing assignments on weekends and at night, plus playing with the band as often as possible. Although still living at home with his family, music was now his only source of income: 'Playing in the band you always get free drinks, and the gigs were pretty regular, so I was able to live okay.' But before long he was obtaining holiday work as a labourer, working for well-known designer and landscaping company, Jenny Smith Gardens. Jim describes Jenny as 'a real stalwart, a practical, hands-on gardener with a great love and knowledge of plants'. Jenny's son Andrew Seccull gave Jim a full-time job after he graduated from Burnley, and he worked for the company for four years. Andrew, who had run the landscaping segment on radio station 3AW for 15 years, taught Jim how to landscape: 'Months and years on the end of a shovel, plus all the practical skills like draining and paving, bricklaying, building a stone wall, laying down a lawn, pruning a rose garden; the lot.'

Finally wanderlust caught up with Jim Fogarty. By this time, most of his mates had completed their courses and gone overseas for a year or two before settling down to their careers. Jim had no ambition to travel overseas, but he thought he might like to see more of Australia. He and his girlfriend travelled to Cairns and arrived in the wet season. Jim seemed to thrive in the hot, moist climate: 'I loved the extremes. Cairns is very much a town built in a rainforest and they're very aware of the environment.' He obtained work with a landscape contractor and learned a lot about gardening in the tropics, as against the cool temperate climate of Melbourne: 'The plants up there are just so different.' But the years of hard, physical work were beginning to have an effect. Long nights playing guitar in the band; swinging an axe in the woodyard and loading tonne after tonne of firewood; travelling long distances on foot with heavy packs in the army; the constant slog of pick and shovel work as a landscaper; they were all beginning to take their toll. Jim had developed that constant scourge of the physical worker—the bad back: 'Even though I was only 25 I was starting to feel it, and wondered whether there was some way of forging some sort of career that didn't involve so much physical work.'

Despite his constantly sore back he was enjoying landscaping in the tropics, but thought, 'There's got to be an easier way to make a living.' His girlfriend had worked in the media in Melbourne and she continued that work in Cairns. Through her Jim had an opportunity to contribute gardening articles to a local publication. He felt he knew enough about tropical gardening to be able to share this information with readers of the magazine *Cairns Life*. He found he had an ability with words and his pieces were well received, but he could never have earned enough to live on. About this time a Hollywood movie, *The Island of Doctor Moreau*, was being filmed near Cairns and Jim obtained work as a non-speaking actor—an 'extra'. Most of his scenes were shot at night and Jim was intrigued by the process: how the sets were built and the location 'dressed' to create a fictional environment; how the camera was used to film a scene, including key shot, reaction shots, reverse angles and so on; the way the microphone 'eavesdropped' on the dialogue. He wondered how you could 'get into landscaping a film set'.

After a year in Cairns, Jim decided to return to Melbourne. By this time his parents were living in Sydney, so he called in on his way through. By now his magazine writing experience and the time he had spent on location with the film crew had whetted his appetite to try something new. He went to Channel 10 in Sydney and met a producer called Karen Wood, who was making a daytime show called *Monday to Friday*, hosted by Bridget Duclos. They were searching for someone to present their weekly gardening segment. Jim looked promising; he taped an audition and was hired. The show was produced in Sydney but Jim was back in Melbourne, so the TV network flew him up every so often and he taped four or five segments at once. In between, he researched and wrote the scripts for these programs. Jim plays down this period: 'It was only day-time TV. It was no big deal. But I learned a lot about television production.' This exposure on commercial TV led to Jim being chosen as one of *Cleo* magazine's most eligible bachelors: 'That was good for a laugh.'

Then suddenly it all came to a near-tragic end. Jim was out with some mates in Melbourne one night when one of them became involved in an argument. 'This young kid—he was obviously on drugs or something—lashed out and smashed a glass in my friend's face and knocked him on his back. Before I knew what was going on, still with the jagged glass in his hand, he whacked me from behind and ripped my whole face open. I didn't feel any pain at the time. But I remember, as each heartbeat seemed to leap out of me, everything went into slow motion; there was blood spraying out of my head. I was just saturated, literally saturated in blood, not knowing what the hell had happened. I nearly lost an eye. An ambulance ride and 28 stitches later, then the whole hospital bit. Before I knew it, I wasn't renewed on the TV show for the coming year. I was back in Melbourne, I was without a job, I didn't know what I was going to do. That was late November. It was the end of the year. So I just took a break.'

Jim suffered a lot of pain from the attack. There were twin lacerations running down his face, beneath his eye and down to his nose. A number of muscles and nerves were severed, the left side of his face was semi-paralysed and he still has a 'lazy eye'. Nor was his pain merely physical: 'My first reaction was anger. I just wanted to go and throttle this kid. It was pretty hard to accept. For the rest of your life your face is going to look all different: scars—train tracks—down my face, and the lazy eye. You find yourself in a situation where you've got no employment and you really don't know what you're going to end up doing. Any heavy impact to the head really knocks you about—especially with all the pain-killers.' Like a wounded dog, Jim headed for home. His family has a holiday house in the seaside village of Flinders, on Westernport Bay and Jim spent most of that summer down there. Days of sand and sun and surf; attempting to recuperate; living on meagre savings that were soon gone: 'I remember going to an ATM and attempting to withdraw $10. That's all I had in the bank. But $10 is below the amount the machine will let you take out, so it refused me my own money! That was probably one of the lowest moments of my life. I only had $10 and I couldn't even get it out of the bank!'

Several years after the attack Jim accepted counselling. He finally knew he had to get the anger out of his system. The trauma of his dreadful experience was continuing to prey on him. He grew short-tempered with friends and family. As a victim of crime he was entitled to free trauma counselling. It helped a lot: 'That was a good feeling, really, to get it off your chest. You learn to forgive, because the other option is to stew over it for the rest of your life. So I just had to forgive what had happened.' Finally, after three years of legal delay, the matter went to court. Jim felt the legal system was skewed against the victim; that he was the one on trial. The offender's barrister accused Jim of being an alcoholic; the judge apologised to the accused because the accused had to undergo a blood test. The young man was found guilty, sentenced to 15 months, 'Suspended though, because he was a first-time offender.'

Jim emerged from that experience determined to make something of his life: 'To try and do something extraordinary.' Trouble was, he didn't know what. Meanwhile he had no work and no money. When a friend asked Jim if he could build him a courtyard, he accepted. It was the first job he'd actually designed: 'I built it out of my head. It was no big deal.' Jim took three months to build the courtyard. 'Very cheap, but six buck's an hour is better than nothing. Landscaping was the only thing I knew.' Jim did that job on his own, but almost before he knew what was happening, he was getting more landscaping jobs. He hired a couple of people, bought an old ute and he was in business.

The Melbourne International Flower and Garden Show was only in its second year at Carlton Gardens when *Your Garden* asked him to build them a show garden. Perhaps his short-lived television exposure had given him some small modicum of fame, or perhaps he was just cheap! The total budget was $5000. In those days the Melbourne show had a different theme each year. In 1998 it was fairytales and fantasies. Jim decided to do something quite different and striking: 'I did a garden with no green. I had a lot of black and silver plants and orange leaves and a black lawn and that sort of stuff, and I got a bronze medal for it.'

Television personality and producer Don Burke filmed this garden as part of his Melbourne show coverage: 'Don was really supportive and he loved that I did something a bit quirky.' He also filmed the courtyard Jim had built for his friend. So almost before Jim knew what was happening he was a fully blown landscape contractor. Within a year or two he had three crews working for him—a total of 12 people. His 1998 *Your Garden* show garden won a bronze medal, and he built another one in 1999 for *Your Garden* which missed out on a medal. In 2000 and 2001 he built displays, which he sponsored, both of which were awarded bronze medals. Jim had developed a taste for medals! 'I got a bit of a hunger. Getting bronze made me hungry. I wanted to learn.' Why couldn't he win silver? Or, better still, gold? One year Julian Dowle, the famed British garden designer, came to Melbourne as a judge at MIFGS. Jim regards Julian as the doyen of garden designers. He asked Julian, 'How can I go beyond bronze?'

Jim now knows that a winning show design must serve a strict set of criteria the judges will relentlessly enforce. Construction must be sound with neat joinery, well-built walls and skilfully laid paving. Plants must be vigorous and true to species and they must appear natural, looking as though they actually grew there. The garden must be perfectly finished, with not a leaf or a blade of grass out of place. But above all else, the completed garden must be absolutely faithful to its original, submitted brief, with absolutely no allowance for variation or modification. It cannot evolve during construction. No last-minute improvements, no second thoughts, no new ideas. If it deviates from its original design brief then the judges will con-clude the designer must have got it wrong in the first place, 'Or someone else may have come along and jazzed it up.' A show garden is the designer's creation, and the finished garden must faithfully reflect its designer's vision.

According to Jim, a show garden has to satisfy all the senses. 'The sense of smell must be served, not only through the perfume of the flowers, but with the sharp tang of rotting earth—of mulch—and the varied, herby, mysterious scents of leaves and other foliage. Sound is generated through the rustle of leaves and—especially—with the trickle or gush or tumbling of water. The tactile sense must be experienced through the imagination: show gardeners frown upon people who actually touch their plants. Multiply your fingers by those of the 135,000 visitors to MIFGS and you can see why. But the textures can be imagined: soft and hard, smooth and rough, silky and coarse, sticky and spongy, prickly and yielding, dry and wet. And not only through the plants but also through such built elements as pavers, water features, wall materials, timber framing, cushion fabrics and even paint. There are also subtle, almost sub-liminal influences: not simply how that tree will look in that posi-tion, but how the shadow of that tree will fall at various times of the day. How a breeze will change the sounds and dynamics of a garden; even how the smoke and cooking smells from an operating barbecue will evoke a domestic connection. All these aspects must be pro-jected from the designer's imagination and calculations onto the drawing board (or computer screen) during early planning.

'With a show garden, it's probably the only time you're actually controlling nature. You've got a nursery growing plants for you and they must be at their best during the week of the show; planned up to a year in advance. You're actually controlling the flowering time of those plants. In a normal garden it mightn't be flowering at that time. Out of 100 plants you're picking the 80 that don't have snail damage, but in a real garden 80 per cent of them would. Doing show gardens gives you a strange, powerful feeling because you know you are playing with nature; every plant is perfect. That's never going to be the case in a real garden. For that split second in time, for the duration of the show, you are dominating nature.'

Designing and building a show garden has nothing to do with building a *real* garden. A show garden is essentially a stage setting, a TV or film set built to create an impression, an illusion that it has been there forever. It is designed to be admired from two, at most three angles; to serve its only purpose, that is, to be critically viewed by an audience for a few days, then to be dismantled and to disappear. Although the built construction may look permanent enough, in reality it is only temporary. Timber features like pergolas, conservatories and summerhouses are built using cheap framing pine and painted with non-permanent paint. Brick and stone walls have been constructed without adequate concrete footings and drainage will be minimal. Even though the plants are real enough and are placed in the show garden in the prime of their life, many will have been planted at their showy, flowering best, usually the wrong time for transplantation. Roots will have been chopped off and many of the plants may still be in pots that have been buried in a bed of mulch. If through some mischance, a show garden were to somehow escape removal, within a year it would be dead, a sad skeleton of brown leaves, withered flowers, weed-smothered beds and dead lawn; its built features now only twisted timberwork, sinking and uneven paving, and sagging—even collapsed—walls.

With the building of a *real* garden, the design will evolve. The designer may choose to modify elements or may need to accommodate changes their client chooses to make; the landscaper may discover difficulties in the concept and other changes may need to be incorporated. But beyond this, the skills and creativity of the designer, landscapers and gardeners only serve but to commence the process. Though their work has been completed the garden is far from finished. Drainage and irrigation systems may have been installed, walls may have been properly constructed, pergolas may have been soundly built, paving may have been expertly laid, and—thanks to the miracle of modern turf—a lawn may be in place. But its trees may be little more than sticks in the ground, shrubs will be small and annuals will be raw beds of spaced out seedlings; tonnes of spread mulch may be the embryo garden's most prominent feature; walls will look new and raw, awaiting the spread of moss and lichen and staining by the weather. There will be few flowers, little shade and certainly no overhead canopy of green foliage, save what may have been originally on the site.

The landscapers will have cleaned up their mess, packed away their tools and departed, leaving it to nature: to the sun, the wind and the rain to complete their work, hopefully assisted by the loving attention, patient weeding and diligent watering of the new garden's proud owners. Before the first few years have passed birds will have flown in, small nocturnal animals may have arrived, children will play cricket on the lawn, barbecue smoke will filter up through leaves. Perhaps, after a decade has gone by, weary home gardeners will sigh, sip a drink, lean back and relax in the shade they believe they have created. Then in 20 years, barring drought, bushfire and wilful neglect, the garden could be looking something like its designer's original vision: a haven of welcoming, comforting green; truly a place to calm the nerves and inspire the soul.

In 2002 Jim Fogarty went into a joint project with a large plant-propagating nursery to create a show garden at MIFGS. Jim would design the garden, the nursery would hire the landscaper and, of course, supply the plants. The budget was adequate and Jim was deter-mined to win a gold medal this time around. Jim was now designing—on paper! 'I still couldn't draw, but I had this great computer guy. He set me up with software so I could draw it all on the computer screen. It was magic.' The design ideas were all Jim's of course, computers do not generate ideas. He did one preliminary draft plan after another and finally he was satisfied. The finished folio of plans was something of which any architect or draughtsman would have been proud.

Before tackling this new show garden, Jim had honed his newly acquired, computer-assisted drafting skills on designs for the TV garden show, *Backyard Blitz*. This show is one of the most successful of the new wave of 'reality' lifestyle programs sweeping Australian television. Each week *Backyard Blitz* transforms an ugly, neglected and often bare backyard into a beautiful, perfectly landscaped, state-of-the art small domestic rear garden, often complete with a water feature and pergola or similar structure; all in two days without the owners knowing a thing about it; and all free of charge. A highlight of each show is the moment when the garden is declared complete and the overjoyed, somewhat embarrassed and usually well-deserving owners are brought in to view their magical new 'dream' environment. The well-known actor or TV personality who anchors the show is its star; the ruggedly attractive, personable young men and women building this 'secret' garden are the 'talent'; and the surprised and delighted owners are the guest performers.

For audience rating reasons, the Channel 9 network decided a certain quota of Melbourne gardens should be fitted into each season. So Don Burke, the owner of the show, suggested the producers should give rising Melbourne garden designer and TV-savvy Jim Fogarty a call. Jim was delighted to face the challenges posed by these projects. The gardens had to be built in two days to a strict budget. The designer had to know something about cameras and how to make a garden look good on camera: 'Colour looks different on camera. You need to go a bit stronger with the colours for TV, otherwise they can look washed out.' A researcher would have followed up 'stories' suggested by viewers, case studies of people thought to be deserving of such special treatment: victims of the Bali bombing, people surviving a major illness. 'People with life stories to tell, often very sad and very tragic.' Jim checked out the backyards, the potential locations—all in secret, of course—and these were then matched against their stories and decisions were made about each proposed Melbourne episode.

While all the other criteria and limitations had to be met, Jim's greatest commitment was to his 'clients', the properties' owners, the people for whom he was really building these gardens, people he would never, under any circumstances, meet. He would endeavour to find out as much about these people as he could: their tastes and interests, likes and dislikes. 'I'm searching for their lifestyle, what style of garden they'd want, then designing something which I hope is quite personal to them.' Jim knows these are show gardens—of a sort. They are exposed on nationwide television to a wider audience, and to greater public scrutiny than any garden at a garden show. But unlike show gardens these must survive. Although constructed in two frenetic days they must live on, bringing their owners joy and contentment across many years. Jim knows that if any aspect of these gardens fails, if in six months trees were dying, structures falling apart, drains blocked or the paving sinking, a scandal could ensue. If this became endemic and rumours of shoddy *Backyard Blitz* landscaping began to circulate, rival TV channels would take great pleasure in publicising these failures on their tabloid-style current affairs programs.

Jim claims he conceived his 2002 MIFGS show garden—the one built in partnership with the nursery—when he'd had a few drinks! He had some problems with the landscaper the client had hired and Jim stood him down. 'I guess to be fair he didn't know what his commitment should have been. He hadn't done a show before.

When you're doing a show garden, Sunday is just another day of work. It's not a day for taking off, because you're putting your reputation on the line for the public.' One night Jim pulled out the front of this garden and decided to rebuild it on his own: 'I thought it'd be easier to do it myself, I'd fix it up.' He still had quite a way to go before the garden was finished. It was about 10 o'clock at night and Jim was working alone, concreting in a wall when Martin Semken and Mark Bence wandered along. Their firm, Semken Landscaping, was building a number of show gardens at MIFGS that year. All of them were virtually finished and Martin and Mark were taking a look around at the other exhibits. They saw Jim working by artificial light and Martin approached and asked him if he wanted any help. 'We've got shovels, we've got blokes, we've got a wheelbarrow. Do you want a hand?' Martin later said, 'Jim looked at me funny and declined.' Jim barely knew Martin or Mark at the time. He knew Semken Landscaping, of which they are principals, was already one of the largest landscaping firms in Victoria. Jim knew his budget for this garden definitely wouldn't run to a gang of Semken people coming onto his site and finishing the job. Besides, there was a certain amount of pride involved. 'I don't offer to help and expect payment,' Martin said. 'It was only 10 o'clock and we could have worked all night. Gratis.' Jim knows that now: 'It was pretty well the first time we'd ever spoken. And I guess being a typical, stubborn Australian you tend to say thanks, but she'll be right. Thanks but no thanks.' So Martin and Mark walked on and Jim finished his garden. When completed, this garden was the talk of the show. It won a gold medal and Jim received the Royal Horticultural Society of Victoria Comeadow Award for Design Excellence.

When his landscaping business was at its peak Jim was employing 12 people working in three crews. But he was far from happy: 'I bloody hated it. I ended up becoming an employment administrator. Instead of doing what I should have been doing, in the garden, I was dealing with superannuation issues, or work cover, or people quitting the job and having to find another worker. I thought, this is crazy. At the end of the year you look at your income, you look at your expenses and expenses often outweigh income. Why do I bother?' Perhaps Jim is too much the perfectionist: 'I had some staff who struggled with that and thought I was a bit too pedantic. I took too much pride in the job. I reckon I underquoted nearly every job because I love gardens. I should have had someone else out there quoting. It all became too personal. When you're dealing with home-owners and their money you feel guilty—and responsible. I had a few situations where I did a deal with someone and it came back to bite me. You know, they didn't pay their last bill and you get a bit used up; taken advantage of. I guess you begin to wise up after a few years of that. A couple of grand's a lot of money when you're in this sort of business and you can hardly take back a garden.'

But Jim had won two major awards with his most recent show garden. Could he have a future working solely as a designer? 'Actually making a living out of just designing is really hard, and even now there's not many people—probably less than 20—who make a living solely out of designing gardens and who don't construct or don't have a nursery.' At a sponsors' lunch following the 2002 Melbourne International Flower and Garden Show, Jim Fogarty sat at a table with the Semken Landscaping team: Martin Semken and Mark Bence. 'It was at the Sofitel or somewhere. It's a small industry and everyone gets on pretty well: a few laughs and a few drinks.' Jim was bemoaning his current position. How he was struggling to survive as a landscaper when all he wanted to do was design gardens. Martin Semken took up the challenge, suggesting Jim would have to decide:

'What are you doing? Are you a designer or are you building gardens?' Jim knew what he wanted to do, and he told them. So Mark Bence responded: 'Well, you can design the gardens and we can build them!' Jim told them he had to consider his staff. He felt obliged to look after them; also he had equipment and several utility trucks. But their tentative offer gave him a lot to think about.

During the months that followed, Jim's relationship with Semken Landscaping grew and the detail in their offer developed. They were prepared to 'buy all the gear and if I was designing maybe I could handball the construction work over their way'. Jim talked this over with his father: 'Dad and I are great mates and I chat a lot with Dad about a lot of things. He always gave me good business advice, especially during the low times, when he used to say, "Why don't you go and get a job in sales somewhere? Company car, superannuation, regular income." But I didn't want to do that.' But when told about the Semken Landscaping offer, Jim's father said, 'Do it. Bite the bullet.' Jim followed this advice. 'Marty, Bency and I settled on an agreed sum, which I felt was pretty fair and reasonable. I was happy just to get rid of it all. There were a lot of old paint tins that were really worth nothing.' According to Martin Semken: 'He had an old bomb ute and a good ute and a few tools and bits and pieces. We took over Jim's construction business and it's been a fantastic relationship since.' Jim made sure each of his employees found another job or moved on to something else. One of them joined Semken Landscaping and is doing well. No one realised it at the time, but the genesis for *Australian Inspiration* was probably born back in May 2002 at that boozy sponsors' lunch.

chapter three

The gardener's apprentice

WHEN MARTIN SEMKEN was growing up his family barely stayed long enough in any one place to begin a garden, let alone to contemplate that Martin might become one of Australia's most successful gardeners. Martin was born into an air force family. 'My dad had been in the RAAF since he was 15 and did an air force apprenticeship in Wagga in New South Wales. He met my mum, Marlene, in Wagga and both my older brother and sister were born there. But being air force you get to move. At the time I was born they were living at Point Cook.' This is an historic air base in Victoria, where many of the original Australian World War I pilots who flew the fabric and matchstick 'kites' in France and Belgium learned to fly. Airman Graeme Semken and his family lived on the base. 'Everyone who lived there was air force,' Martin remembers. The base had its own primary school, 'It was a classic old schoolhouse, like in a country town. If you were left-handed you got your hand tied behind your back so you'd write right-handed. My big brother Stephen was my hero. He used to get the strap.' The family moved back to Wagga for a while before shifting back to Victoria, to the air force base at Laverton, also near Melbourne.

'We didn't live on the base at Laverton, we lived in a Housing Commission house. I know Housing Commission conjures up different thoughts in different people, but as a kid it was a great place to live; it was a community. We were all air force or army or navy and they were all great people. We wouldn't have thought of living anywhere else; I thought it was heaven to live in the Housing Commission. And I have fond memories of Laverton: one of them is of a huge fir tree out the back, a cypress, 60 to 70 feet high. I used to climb to the top and grab hold of a branch and ride it like I was riding a horse, then I'd fall and grab the next branch and ride these branches all the way down until I fell the last eight or ten feet.' Watching the aeroplanes passing low overhead, Martin convinced himself he could fly: 'I jumped off the shed roof. I waved my arms really hard and I landed with no air left in my lungs.'

After a brief stint in the United States—where Graeme Semken was training to fly the new F-111 fighter aircraft—the Semkens returned to Australia. Graeme was posted to Melbourne, to a position at Victoria Barracks in St Kilda Road, and the family was allocated a Housing Commission house in the suburb of Broadmeadows. 'No problem for me. I didn't know Broadmeadows wasn't a nice place. I thought it was a great place. I went to Upfield High and played footy and just enjoyed life there. Dad was now in an office job and I don't know that he liked that, I think he liked it better out on the base. Not long after that Dad left the air force and we moved to Ringwood. That was the end of a major chapter in my life: the travelling. If you added it up, I'd been to 13 different schools in 14 years; I'd start at a new school and I'd have to fill in a form listing the previous schools I'd attended—I'd have to ask for another sheet of paper.' Martin's business has always been based at Ringwood, in the eastern suburbs of Melbourne, and Martin has lived there ever since. 'We lived in Mitcham for a year while the house was built in Ringwood. An A.V. Jennings house in an estate. Mum and Dad were very proud of that house—we'd never owned a house. They loved picking the tiles; they'd never had a choice of anything before. We just got what we got. I don't think we owned a new anything up until then. Mum and Dad bought a new refrigerator and they've still got it. My dad bought a new car. It was a Holden Monaro, the first one out.'

Martin enrolled at Norwood High School in North Ringwood. 'I felt at home there. For the first time I had a base in my life. To be a nomad and then have a base; it's a totally different feeling.' Martin remembers his first meeting with Mark Bence. 'I walked into that school ground for the first time, on my first morning at that school, and I looked around. I could walk up and say, "Hi, I'm Marty." Or "Martin", or whoever I decided to be. That's one thing about going to new schools, you could re-invent yourself. So things you didn't like about yourself, you could think, "Well, maybe I won't be that bloke this year." So I looked around and I saw these four guys playing handball, which I'd never seen before. They had stupid long hair down to their waists and one of them was Mark Bence. Mark had some common interests with me and we became mates. Mark and I did biology together, and Mark did economics and I didn't, which is probably why he runs the business and I still get my hands dirty. Our real friendship started to develop when we played cricket together at North Ringwood. We were both left-arm bowlers and we really loved cricket, and we threw ourselves at it. We had a famous moment when Mark took six wickets for 24 runs, and I took four wickets for 23 in the one match. We bowled the opposition out without anyone else bowling a ball.

'We were more than just schoolmates. A good friend died in a car accident when we were all 18, and that was a part of our journey in life that changed Mark and I forever. We reached Year 12 together and did our Higher School Certificate. Some kids had gone by then, but Mark and I stuck it out. I'd like to say that both of us were a lot more intelligent than we let anyone know. We'd get an "A" for something then two weeks later we'd get an "E". We just didn't care much. There were other things in life that made more sense.' Neither Mark nor Marty were seriously contemplating university. 'We had a careers teacher at Norwood High. She hit a nerve with me, a nerve that has been rough-ended ever since. I wasn't a high achiever at school, but I knew I could get a "B" in any subject I wanted. I knew I was going to make it and just get over the line. She suggested I should get a job in a bank. That would have been a great career back then. You could get a job as a clerk in a bank and work your way up and one day be a bank manager. I told her I was actually thinking of working outside, maybe as a gardener. She said, "Martin, you've got a problem. You've got Peter Pan syndrome." I didn't know what she was talking about. But what she meant was, Peter Pan is the little boy who never grows up. Go and get your hands dirty, playing in the sandpit; you're never going to grow up. And I thought, "If that's what I'm going to be, I want to get a job I enjoy, and my mum will be proud of me. I'll be a gardener and I'll achieve for the rest of my life." Actually that career teacher did a great job. I thank her nearly every day of my life.'

Perhaps believing he needed to combine some sort of academic career with his ambition to work outside, Martin applied to enter Dookie Agricultural College to do a diploma course. 'It seemed like the only opening. There weren't careers in environmental science or ecology then, there was just Dookie.' Dad and I drove up there in the pouring rain so I could do a written test. We got a flat tyre. I got in to the course and I deferred; I wanted to keep my options open. I don't think I ever told them I wasn't coming. Perhaps they're still holding a place for me!' Knowing what he knows now, Martin is glad he didn't go to Dookie: 'Kids who came from the city and went through Dookie were lucky to get a job. It was never a career path. If your father owned a farm it was different.' Martin had had almost nothing to do with gardens or gardening, but the job still beckoned. Marlene Semken found three newspaper advertisements announcing gardening apprenticeships: one with the Melbourne and Metropolitan Board of Works, one with the City of Nunawading and another with the City of Ringwood. 'The Board of Works had a great apprenticeship program, the City of Nunawading was really going ahead horticulturally, and Ringwood was my home town. I applied for all three.' As an occupation, landscape gardening was becoming quite popular, but most beginner apprentices were aged 15 or 16. 'To be applying for an apprenticeship after Year 12 was pretty odd. I did an aptitude test at the Board of Works. Then I did it at Nunawading. Same test! The bloke from Nunawading rang me up and said, "We've been running this test for years now, and you've got the highest score ever. So we think you're over-qualified for the apprenticeship—we're not going to interview you."'

Martin was interviewed by Alan Robertson, the city engineer at Ringwood. Robertson later became their first chief executive officer, and Martin considers him 'the father of the City of Ringwood. He took it from a country town to a thriving metropolis. This big man—he was a huge man, he played footy—interviewed me in this big office. He would have interviewed 50 or 60 kids for the job. Then a little later, at about tea-time at our house, there was a knock at the door and this huge man was at the door. He'd come to meet my mum and dad and offer me an apprenticeship. He believed an apprenticeship was more than just a job, it was a commitment. He wanted to know who my mum and dad were and to offer me the job in person. To this day, that's how we offer apprenticeships to kids.' Martin and Mark visit the young people in their homes and meet their parents. Semken Landscaping have won the Victorian Apprentice Employer of the Year Award twice, once in horticulture and once across all trades. 'We still regard an apprenticeship as a commitment to each other. You sign indentures; that creates a commitment between an apprentice and an employer. You believe in each other. It's a great system.' Martin is proud to have been an apprentice and to be able to give other young people that opportunity. One of Semken Landscaping's former apprentices is going to Chelsea with the team. 'Paul Stammers—he started with us. He had long hair down to his waist. Now I think he's the premier landscaper in Australia. He's not just a gardener, he's a stonemason, he's everything. A few years ago Alan Robertson rang me up and said, "Martin, I want you to come and build my garden for me." That was a proud moment.'

'I was lucky to be at Ringwood, which was still expanding. They were still building new parks and ovals,' and the maintenance load was steadily growing. But they still harked back to the old ways: 'They still had a horse and dray and horse-drawn rollers. If I'd gone to one of the inner suburbs, they'd already have changed to the modern era. We didn't have computers, we didn't have radios and as a young kid I worked with blokes who'd been to the Second World War. They taught me how to drive, how to back a trailer, how to use a chainsaw. It was a really hands-on apprenticeship.' Martin did well at trade school: 'For the first time ever I got a bit of success. I was doing what I wanted to do and I really worked hard at school and I worked hard on the job. But I have to give my mum credit—she used to help me with all my homework. Suddenly I had something to talk to older people about. Here was this 20-year-old kid who knew what was wrong with their hydrangea! Gardening's the most popular hobby in the world, and I get to do it for a job. I wake up every day and think how good that is.' Martin completed his apprenticeship in three years; not the usual four, 'But because I'd done HSC and for the first time in my life excelled at school, I got an early release.' Martin averaged over 89 per cent for 24 subjects across the three years of his trade schooling.

Late in Martin's apprenticeship Peter Rashleigh was made superintendent of parks and gardens. 'He was a real go-getter. He'd been employed by the City of Springvale and he had new ideas, new energy. He wanted everyone to know that Ringwood wasn't a country bumpkin town; it was a modern, growing city. I was lucky enough to ride that wave of energy. He brought out the best in me. Graham Marriott was brought in as assistant superintendent. Graham was also a great influence on my working life. He was the hardest man and the fairest man. He also had an ability to bring you down to earth. By now I've been five years at the job and I'm probably 22 and pretty unbreakable; cheeky as buggery and pretty much knew everything. One morning Graham Marriott said to me, "Come on, we're going to pour a concrete floor in a shed." I turned round to him and said, "Listen, Graham, I'm a gardener, mate, not a concreter. You get one of the labourers to do that." So he grabbed me by the back of the neck and said, "You'll come and pour concrete floors, and you'll muck in the concrete until I tell you you're a gardener!" Now, 20-odd years on, for the first five or 10 years with Semken Landscaping, I reckon I made more money pouring concrete than being a gardener. So I went and poured concrete and at the end of the day he bought me a chocolate milkshake with malt. Be a lot of things, I learned, but don't be a smart aleck. Now I know that at the end of a tough day the right thing to do is go and buy a beer or a Coke or a chocolate milkshake and share it. Graham's the best gardener I ever met.

'I'd been made Parks Officer by then, which meant I was third in charge. I did some great projects with young kids. They had something called the RED scheme, with long-term unemployed, and they worked on government-funded projects. I managed quite a few of those and really loved them. I learned how to manage people and work better with people.' Martin was satisfied to stay at Ringwood while he was learning his trade, but he always wanted to be the boss. 'I realised that Graham and Peter weren't going anywhere, and being third in charge probably wasn't me. I'd been there seven years, so I applied for a job at Presbyterian Ladies' College as head gardener. That sounded like a pretty good job, to be head gardener at one of Melbourne's big private schools. I went there with heaps of energy, ready to change the world. But I'd never worked at the same place every day. At Ringwood I'd worked at the golf course or the ovals or one of the parks; we had new projects every day. I had seven gardeners under me, so it was great experience, but that careers teacher probably had me right: I had to be on the move. So for the first time ever I wanted out. There was a head carpenter who told the gardeners what to do, and I didn't like that; there were a lot of politics in the place. So after 18 months I decided to move on.'

He applied for a job at the City of St Kilda as assistant superintendent. 'It was a whole new world. I'd come from Ringwood, which was a suburban bush environment with annuals, and here I was going to a real multicultural environment with a seaside aspect.' As well as broadening his social attitude, Martin knew his horticultural knowledge would be expanded. 'It was a developing council with all sorts of new ideas. So I went to St Kilda with 54 staff and one boss. But for the first time I realised I was doing someone else's work and he was getting all the credit. I loved the people and I loved the place, but I didn't like that. The boss always made changes at the last minute. So I learned a new management style: management by impact. I had learned about management by care, management by example, management by being tough, management by being fair. But this guy had a new skill. You could do nothing for a week, then come in at the last minute and make changes. Then everyone would see you as a manager: management by impact. It was a negative form of management, one I hated and resented. By now I'd been in the workforce for 10 years, and I thought becoming superintendent of parks was a great career. But already some councils were joining together, amalgamating, and I thought that maybe this isn't such a great career.' The number of available senior positions was shrinking. 'Some of the councils were getting bigger and had a director of parks: a guy who wore a suit. I was going to be the youngest superintendent—the youngest director, then I got a glimmer of the future. I didn't think, "Oh yeah, this is all going to fall apart." But I just felt there was a difference developing.'

On top of his regular job Martin had been working 'for himself' for years. Even when he was an apprentice at Ringwood people would approach him in the street and offer him weekend work trimming trees or mowing lawns; even laying paving. He usually brought his mate Mark Bence in on these projects and they began building a little business. This continued after Martin finished his apprenticeship and left Ringwood: 'Through all of this I was working weekends and holidays for myself. We'd take on jobs we should never have done. I remember cutting down this massive tree in Ringwood. We hired a cherry picker, a travel tower. I borrowed a chainsaw from the council.' The tree fell the wrong way. 'We worked hard and sweated hard. We worked long days. We worked at night. We used to say that if we didn't take a hangover to work on Sunday morning then we weren't having fun in life. Sunday morning, everyone else would be sleeping in, but Mark and I would be up at 6.30am and going to the job. Plenty of times I'd jump into Mark's old Landrover and I hadn't even been to bed. But we could afford to buy things none of our friends owned. When we went to buy a stereo, Mark and I, we'd buy one each. We owned the biggest stereos. We learned to work. We learned to love it. We did a huge landscaping job in Nunawading, and another one out at Greensborough; weekend after weekend. But at the end of each day we had a hundred bucks each. We enjoyed it. Simple as that: we enjoyed it.'

Martin left the security of the City of St Kilda and his place well up the ladder of a council career, plunging headlong into the world of small business: full-time and alone. He was married with one child when he took the leap. His drop in take-home pay was massive.

'I was assistant superintendent with a car. I hadn't had to own a car for years. Always had a council car, council fuel. I'd spent nine years building a career in a structure that had been around forever.' But within a few years the whole municipal horticultural bureaucracy had disintegrated. 'I jumped off the ship just before it sank.' Martin's decision to go out on his own was largely influenced by an offer made to him by the owners of Aquafield. 'They supplied watering systems for gardens, public parks and sports fields. I knew them from working at the City of Ringwood. They were leaders in the irrigation industry and they said, "You go out on your own and we'll give you work; any day you don't have work, come and see us."'

As assistant superintendent at St Kilda council, Martin had more than 50 people working for him. He had no call to work physically in the field. 'I was well finished with the tools, so to go back to the grassroots and be a one-man show was a huge step. Semken Landscaping began in October 1987, the day the stock market crashed. Aquafield said, "Here's a job, go and do it." They gave me the stuff and the address and the layout and I headed off out there. Then I thought, "Hang on, I'll never get through this. I need a bloke to dig the holes and I'll lay the pipe." That was on the Monday and on the Friday night I employed my first staff member.' Martin has adhered to an ironclad philosophy right through his business life: never refuse a contract, never knock back a job. By April the following year, six months later, there were three of them—Martin and two employees—and they were overwhelmed with work. So he asked Mark Bence to come in with him—as an equal partner. 'I sold half of Semken Landscaping to Mark for a trailer and a slab of beer. It was a good sale, though I've heard Mark wants half the slab of beer back! And it wasn't that good a trailer, actually, although we've still got it.' When Martin went out on his own, despite the stock market crash, he didn't realise he was taking a risk. 'It never dawned on me that it was a big move until April 11, 1988, when Mark joined the business. Mark had a great job at Telstra; he was really going places. I went to bed that night and for the first time in my whole working life, I couldn't get to sleep. I thought, "What if I've done this wrong? Why did I inflict this on Mark? What if we can't pay the bills?" But I never lost sleep again, and I'm never going to.

'I had two staff members and myself and Mark made four. I had a ute and Mark had a ute and we had Mark's trailer. There are those days when I'm sure Mark and I hate each other, but I've yet to have an argument with him, so I suppose we know when one should win and one should lose. You know when to give in. Mark and my dad— my dad used to work with us—wanted a cement mixer. It was going to cost $1000. I said, "Can't we make the mud in a wheelbarrow?" Then they wanted this brick cutter. We used to cut bricks with an angle grinder. They wanted to spend a couple of thousand dollars on this brick cutter. I thought that we'd just go broke with these two, the way they want to keep spending money. But we bought the brick cutter and we've still got it and it's made its money, so I'm happy with that decision.' And they've still got the cement mixer. 'We even got a bank loan to buy our first two mobile phones—they cost us $3000 each!'

Martin had learned a solid lesson at St Kilda council. He saw that management by impact, by chaos, ultimately failed. He knows there is more to employing someone than simply giving them a job. 'If you're not interested in their life, you won't know why they're having a good day or a bad day. It's not just being their boss.' The interest Mark and Martin show in their apprentices extends to all their people, and they (and their wives) attend their workers' weddings and engagement parties, their 21st birthdays and their football club presentation nights. Martin says, 'They're part of the family.' Semken Landscaping isn't managed through impact, but through example and care for people. They also continue to accept every job that comes their way. 'So we've just kept employing people and buying utes.' Now Martin claims they are probably the biggest private landscaping company in Australia, employing 75 people. 'We're big champions of self-belief. So we've decided we're the biggest landscape employer in Australia. If someone said, "No you're not", then fair enough. But it sounds good on our CV so it'll do for us. That's how we've been with everything: say yes, then worry about how. If you say no, you'll never know.' They call Semken Landscaping 'Shit Yeah Landscaping' around the trade. 'Can you do that?' they ask. 'Shit yeah we can,' is the reply.

'Robbie Phillips was a great part of Semken Landscaping. He owns his own company now, and we're pretty proud of Robbie. Somebody would ask, "Can you do this?" and Robbie would say, "We haven't done one of those for a while, but yeah, we'll be right with that." We still say that to people. "Can you build this 10-metre high waterfall feature?" We say, "We haven't done one for a while." That means, "We've never done one, but we're not going to let anyone else know that." We haven't done a garden at Chelsea for a while either, but I'm sure we'll be all right.'

chapter four

Searching for gold

MARK BENCE, THE second half of Semken Landscaping, has lived all his life in Warrandyte. This is an old goldmining town on the Yarra River that sprawls along a beautiful valley and through the timbered ridges in the hills beyond Melbourne. He is a fifth generation descendent of Tom Logan, who took out a licence to mine gold at Warrandyte in 1852. Mark grew up surrounded by his extended family in a community on the edge of the bush, a community that faced the recurring threat of fires and even floods. It was a community that looked after itself, created its own entertainment, celebrated its togetherness and defended its independence. During the railway boom of the 1880s and 1890s a steel cobweb spread out from Melbourne creating residential suburbs along its length, and such a railway was planned to go through Warrandyte. But the Yarra Valley rated a low priority in the corridors of colonial government, and an economic depression intervened before this could happen. Warrandyte remained isolated, served in later years by a spasmodic bus service. These ingredients could have created a bucolic, gossip-ridden, insular backwater, but several factors saved Warrandyte from this fate. In 1851 it was hailed as the site of the first official gold discovery in Victoria, and although it was never a successful field it provided a meagre living for several generations of staunch, independently minded working men.

A second important infusion into the Warrandyte population took place at the beginning of the 1900s and was a direct result of the railway *not* arriving. The 1890s was a decade of great political and cultural ferment in Australia. The six colonies were squabbling their way towards Federation, and such writers as Henry Lawson and A.B. 'Banjo' Paterson were household names. Visual artists were also stretching their canvases and their talent and were working towards a truly Australian style, experimenting with impressionist paintings that glowed with clean bright light and pioneering vitality, in strong contrast to the work of their European artistic forebears, who mistakenly saw the country through mist-shrouded eyes. These artists worked and lived in various locations, but they became known as the 'Heidelberg School'; Heidelberg is located downriver from Warrandyte. It was then a small town, but when the railway came and a suburb began developing, many of the artists abandoned the place and fled upriver to Warrandyte. In the century since, many artists—painters, potters, sculptors, writers—have settled in Warrandyte, but the place has never seen itself as an artists' colony; the community has remained comfortably integrated. A number of intellectuals and professionals have also moved in, attracted by the lifestyle, the landscape and the benefits of such an open community. You may have a plumber living on one side of you, a poet on the other and a nuclear physicist over the back fence. It was among the children of such people that Mark Bence spent his childhood.

Mark Bence's mother Wilma was directly descended from Tom Logan. Her father, William Hussey, operated a quarry in South Warrandyte. He also ran the coach service from Ringwood railway station, driving a two-horse open drag up and down the hilly, unpaved roads in all weathers, through Warrandyte and beyond to Templestowe and Heidelberg. He is immortalised as 'Ben Hussey', the drag driver who took the girls to their picnic at Hanging Rock in Joan Lindsay's novel and Peter Weir's film. Joan Lindsay came to Warrandyte as a young student painter, usually travelling from Ringwood in William Hussey's drag. Mark's father Bruce also had a country background. He grew up on a dairy farm at Werribee South, not far from Melbourne. It was Bruce Bence who introduced Mark to the bush, and ultimately to the Australian wilderness. Although Bruce Bence spent most of his formal working life indoors, he was a true bushman. 'He worked for Telecom, but I think he was a bushman at heart,' Mark remembers. 'In some ways he was an environmentalist, long before it was fashionable. He spent a lot of his spare time in the bush and instilled that into us as very young kids. He was a keen bushwalker. Grandad (William Hussey) was also a real bushman, I suppose. Dad enjoyed nothing better than working out in Grandad's paddock in South Warrandyte.'

Bruce passed his appreciation of the natural world to his sons, Stephen and Mark. 'Stephen's still a very keen bushwalker. I'd been going on bushwalks with Dad, day walks or overnight, since I was five or six. But my first real bushwalk was for three nights down at Wilson's Promontory. I would've been 11 or 12 at the time. It was one of those things I always desperately wanted to do, because most years we took Dad out to Essendon Airport and he flew over to

Tasmania to go walking through Cradle Mountain–Lake St Clair National Park. I still find one of the most enjoyable things you can do is to go walking through the bush for a week. Most people look at you strangely when you say that. It's very relaxing, because you get away from all the pressures of modern life.' Mark walked though Cradle Mountain–Lake St Clair when he was 13. 'It's a solid walk: 52 miles, 80 kilometres. I did that six times between the ages of 13 and 21. And Bruce being Bruce, you couldn't walk past a mountain without climbing it, so you didn't just walk the 52 miles, you virtually climbed up and down every mountain you passed. Every view is different, so it didn't matter how many times you'd climbed that mountain, you still had to climb it again. That's one of the great appreciations we learned: natural areas change all the time—cloud patterns, different weather, even different climates.' The Bences always walked through Cradle Mountain in February–March. 'The first year there was a drought and very little water—you had to carry it all with you. While there were streams, there was very little other water around. The following year it rained every day and we were in melting snow. Same place, same time of year, just 12 months later. Bruce understood those things very well, and he certainly passed them on to us.'

But for Bruce Bence the outdoors was not just a place to enjoy yourself; it was also a place in which to work. 'Thinking back to Warrandyte in the 1970s and 1980s, it was just a village. My grandmother lived across the road, Molly Logan lived next door to us, and then there was Aggie Moore and Mrs Moore—all elderly ladies. Bruce used to do a lot of work for them, all around the community, and I used to go and help him: mowing lawns and chopping down trees. And he was a hard taskmaster; we had to do it right. So you're up at the crack of dawn and you work until dark. Didn't matter if you were six or 16, you worked flat out all day. I learned all those bushworking and gardening skills from him. Bruce was a frustrated bushworker, but he had a nice balance in his life. I think if it hadn't been for his family commitments he would have loved to have been a national park ranger. He was always a keen volunteer member of the Country Fire Authority in Warrandyte, and in the end he found his perfect job. In the late 1960s he became a trainee regional officer with the CFA. Then he became assistant communications officer, responsible for telephones and alarms. That combined one of his passions in life—the CFA—with his training as a technician.' In his retirement, after suffering serious heart trouble, Bruce took to researching and writing local history. He wrote many monographs, culminating in a book detailing the history of firefighting in the Warrandyte district, one the most fire-prone areas in the world.

Mark Bence first met Martin Semken at Norwood High School, North Ringwood, early in the school year of 1974. It was an important meeting, a meeting that changed the course of both their lives, though neither would have imagined it at the time. 'Marty rolled up and we became very good mates.' They began spending a lot of time together out of school, even though they lived some distance apart; so it was mainly weekend stopovers. 'I got to know Marty's mum and dad very well, and he got to know mine. I think we both saw each other's folks as a second set of parents. We took Martin to the southern end of Cradle Mountain–Lake St Clair once. We must have been about 21. We went into the bottom end of Lake St Clair and up into an area called The Labyrinths and spent a week camping there. Martin's very fit but I think it was quite a culture shock for him. The food is very different and the lifestyle is very different when you're out bushwalking. After you've cooked the evening meal and you've strained off the water you've cooked the peas in, you don't throw it away, you drink it out of cups. Martin will never forget that. He still talks about drinking the "pea juice"!'

When Mark left high school at the end of Year 12 he started work with A.W. Allen, the confectionery firm, with a view to becoming an apprentice fitter and turner in their maintenance engineering department. 'The most important thing I learned there was that I didn't want to become a fitter and turner.' Mark had also done an entrance exam for Telecom. 'After a few months I got a call from Telecom, asking me if I wanted to come in for an interview. I already knew fitting and turning wasn't for me, so I went in to the interview. I then joined Telecom as a trainee in sales administration.' At first, Mark wasn't too sure about that job either. 'I'd probably always wanted to work outdoors, out in the bush, and at some stage I'd had aspirations of becoming a park ranger. That was probably Bruce's influence. But I hadn't really done the right subjects and I probably hadn't worked hard enough. Anyway, I started at Telecom on the sales administration side and I really enjoyed it. I enjoyed talking to people and helping people. It was a job that suited me at the time. Anyway, I spent 10 years at it. Most of my work with Semken Landscaping is now administration and managerial, so those years have proved enormously valuable.

'I began as a sales clerk and then I ran sales teams and a crew of four people. I worked for eight months in Telecom shops in the suburbs and managed the Telecom shop in Greensborough.' Mark's success in sales encouraged Telecom to use him in a training role, finally promoting him to manager of their State Commercial Training Centre. Everyone who knows Mark knows he possesses a wonderful capacity to get on with people. 'In Telecom, I realised I enjoyed the fellowship of the teams; I enjoyed the social interaction.' But the organisation was changing, it was being privatised and Mark had been transferred to running a large telemarketing team. Here the staff were attempting to sell things to people who probably didn't want to talk on the phone, let alone buy something. 'They were doing a job, they were getting paid for it, but it was just a job. They didn't believe in it. And it's a lousy job. We were under pressure to meet certain sales targets, yet I couldn't make any decisions on how I thought I could improve sales.' When Mark suggested a solution to deal with all the paperwork, his idea got stuck in the bureaucracy. 'I wanted to improve the system. Whether it would have been successful or not I don't know, because I didn't stay long enough to find out.'

During the 10 years Mark worked at Telecom he had been going out on weekends and holidays working with Martin. Mainly landscaping, laying paving and building retaining walls, but they'd do pretty well anything that came their way. 'It didn't matter what the weather was like, we'd get out there and just do it. I learned that from Bruce, too. Sometimes I thought that Bruce was terribly harsh, but I suppose I can sit back 30 years later and know I learned all these things from him, and when Martin started picking up these jobs, I already had a lot of skills.' Mark enjoyed getting out in the open air at weekends and working with Marty, but the main motivation was the money. 'We're going back to the late 1970s, early 1980s. Marty and I could earn $100 for a day's work. When Martin started his gardening apprenticeship he was earning $42 a week. I was earning $59 as a fitting and turning apprentice and had a massive pay rise to $112 a week when I went to Telecom. So to go out and do a day's work—and we worked hard for it—and earn $100, was just enormous money. And I enjoyed it. It was easy to go and do it, because I actually enjoyed doing it, and at the end of the day they'd hand me those dollar notes.'

At times Martin and Mark talked about Mark leaving Telecom and making landscaping his career. 'We discussed it. How one day we should set up our own landscaping business because we reckoned we'd do all right at it. But it was always the same thing. At that stage we were probably 23 or 24. We were both married and paying off mortgages on houses. So while we thought that we're good at this and we could probably do it, it was a big step from the thought to the reality—to actually make a living and support our families.' While Mandy, Mark's wife, and Anne, Martin's wife, were both working, 'It was still a big step. We knew we should do it, but I suppose it was one those things that everyone talks about but never does.' Finally Martin made the big decision, and with the backing of Aquafield set up Semken Landscaping and went out on his own. 'The night before he started we went to a Mexican restaurant in Lower Plenty and he talked about it. He was reasonably nervous, but it was an opportunity and he had a reasonable guarantee from Aquafield that they'd give him work.' There was no talk that night about Mark joining Martin in this venture. Martin knew that Mark had a secure, executive position at Telecom. He probably realised it would be difficult enough supporting one young family off this seemingly risky enterprise, let alone two. Mark may have been quietly envious of the big step his best mate was taking, but Martin did it alone; at least for the time being.

This one-man business—Semken Landscaping—quickly became a three-man business, and when Martin landed his largest subcontract to that time, this ultimately led to Mark and Martin's partnership. It began as an extended weekend's work. On behalf of Aquafield Martin took on the task of installing automatic watering systems throughout a new, three-acre garden. 'It was October–November, the peak of the irrigation season.' There was a landscaper—with whom the owner was becoming increasingly dissatisfied—attempting to build the garden Martin was irrigating. 'He was trying to landscape three acres by himself and he was going nowhere. So the owner of the place asked Marty if he could do the landscaping.' And Marty being Marty replied, 'Sure I can.' Marty's team of three had enough to do, laying this extensive irrigation system during the week, 'So Marty came to me and said, "Do you want to work every weekend?" Martin organised all his mates and over a two or three month period we landscaped this three-acre property. The job turned out very well, which wasn't a bad effort, considering the skill base we had for such a big job. Everyone was getting the daily rate, but I was getting a little more. I was like Marty's site foreman because we'd done all these weekend jobs together.'

Martin was still following his principle of never refusing a job, so inevitably the business was growing. One evening he asked Mark, 'Look, do you want to come into a partnership? I've got too much work, I wouldn't mind a partner, do you want to come and work with me?' For Mark it was exactly the right moment. 'Marty knew my circumstances at the time—Mandy was pregnant with Claire (their first child)—so I knew he thought that if I was going to do it, it would be as a partnership; I wasn't just going to be an employee. Anyway, Marty wanted it like that. He knew I was in a situation at Telecom where I was frustrated. The timing was right as I'd had a gutful of dealing with people at Telecom. After Marty had asked me I went home and talked to Mandy and the next day I said yes. As well as the Telecom situation, the outdoor work was certainly appealing. And the fact that Martin had a subcontract with Aquafield meant they would be providing us with enough work. I thought that we were going to bring in an income. There was some guarantee we were going to be paid every day, even if it wasn't as much as I was getting at Telecom. I tried to get a package from Telecom but they weren't giving packages to 28-year-old managers. Martin asked me in late January, early February, but I waited until my 10-year long service leave was due in April and I joined Semken Landscaping on April 11, 1988.' Martin offered to change the name of the company to Semken–Bence. 'First thing Marty offered. Straight off, he said, "We'll change the name of the company." But I just didn't have a problem. Martin had 10 years experience in the horticultural industry, and he had most of the contacts. He offered several times, but it just didn't bother me. I don't hang my hat on that sort of stuff. It seemed to make good business sense to use the same name.'

At the beginning of Mark and Martin's partnership they had a labour force of four: themselves and two workmen. 'I tended to do the "hard" landscaping such as paving and bricklaying, and Martin tended to do more of the "soft" landscaping such as planting and soil mulching. Then when we started doing garden maintenance, Martin used to run the maintenance. So we probably always had different roles within the company. As the company grew and we had a few more people, Martin was the first one off the tools. He'd go out and do the quotes and I'd run the jobs. But we could always do the other one's job, if we had to.' Mark had to learn a number of skills beyond lopping trees and digging trenches: 'I could swing a shovel,

I could dig holes, but I had to lay paving, install water features, construct stone and brick walls. I'm a shocking brickie! You wouldn't want to pay me by the hour as a bricklayer!' Mark had to learn timber construction as well: building pergolas and carports. Martin's father Graeme Semken, who worked with them from time to time, was a proficient handyman and able to build practically anything. '"Pop" Semken was very good. He taught me a lot of that stuff—carports and pergolas—so Pop and I used to go and build them.

'In the early days we did everything and anything. We hand-dug graves at the Warrandyte cemetery for a while.' If they had to dig a grave in a position where they couldn't use a machine, they'd call in Marty and Mark and they'd dig it. 'We were the on-call team that would go in and hand-dig graves because no one else was prepared to do it. Anything and everything; that's a philosophy we've carried through to the present day.' Their method of expansion has always been 'put on some more blokes and buy another ute'. But they have never indulged in large capital investments. They own no big tip-trucks or heavy earthmoving machinery, just utility trucks, lawn-mowers, cement mixers, chainsaws and gardening tools. 'We've always seen ourselves as gardeners. We never wanted to become tip-truck drivers. You buy big machinery, and if you don't have it working five or six days a week, it doesn't pay for itself. We've always followed the principle that if you're going to do a job and you need an excavator, we'll put that price into the job and we'll hire the excavator to go and do the job. Neither of us is mechanical, so it never interested us to have big machinery. There's plenty of blokes out there who want to hire you machines. We went down the line that you should keep your overheads down to a reasonable level, then, if things get hard it's easier to make ends meet.'

As the company has grown both in size and scope, Martin and

Mark have tended to concentrate on separate roles: Mark as administration manager and Martin as construction manager. Martin runs the jobs, Mark runs the company. Mark and Martin have been best mates for 30 years, workmates for 26 years and business partners for 16 years. 'While we've got a lot in common, we're also very different. Martin comes up with lots of ideas and gung-ho things to do, and I'm probably fairly conservative. Martin's ideas are often "out there" while I probably sit back and analyse things; Marty draws the big picture and I fill it in. We complement each other; we understand each other pretty well; we rarely have disagreements. If one of us feels strongly or passionately about something, the other one will sit there and weigh it up and make a conscious decision. Are we going to have a fight about this one, or just let it ride? Sometimes we're not sure, but if we think the other one's passionate about this, we'll give it a ride and see what happens.' Sometimes it works, sometimes it doesn't. 'But we don't make an issue of it. If one of us wants to go in a certain direction, the other will support him, and if it doesn't quite work, well, it was worth a try and let's move on to the next thing.'

Mark had learned his bush-working skills from his father, landscaping skills from Martin and woodworking skills from Graeme Semken. He had also spent 10 years with Telecom acquiring 'people' skills and experience in sales and business administration. But he was now working in the horticultural profession, and was taking an increasingly leading role in that industry. So as their business was growing and they were employing and training more people, Mark felt a need to undergo some solid professional training. Perhaps he needed to keep ahead of their apprentices! He enrolled at Burnley Horticultural College and completed an Advanced Certificate of Horticulture. 'Took me four and a half years at night school.' He studied botany, garden design, landscaping engineering, drainage and soil science. Before this study he knew how to do things; increasingly he was now learning why you did things. Theory now explained and illuminated his practical experience, and scientific understanding strengthened his knowledge of the natural world. Many of the skills he'd picked up along the way were developed and systematised, many of the plants he'd used and come to know were given Latin names. 'It's now the equivalent of Certificate IV. It's a step between what an apprentice does as their formal training and a Diploma of Horticulture.'

Semken Landscaping has been building show gardens at the Melbourne International Flower and Garden Show for eight years. Mark Bence built their first one: 'Actually two of us built our first show garden—David 'Charlie' Brown and I. It was the second year MIFGS was at Carlton Gardens. Martin was on holidays. We were contracted by a firm called Danks, who own the Plants Plus group. The guy who ran Danks's horticultural section, Peter Van Dyke, used to work at Warranglen in Warrandyte. He got us to build it.' It was hardly a garden—more a floral display within a large marquee. It was erected to accommodate speakers on gardening topics and their audiences, with banks of flowers at the entrance. 'So it was paving and planting and Charlie and I went and built it.' Mark acknowledges that show gardens have proved very important to the prestige of the company and to the morale of everyone who works for them. 'We've probably built 20 show gardens at MIFGS. We did seven in 2003 and we're doing five in 2004.' Mark agrees with Martin that there is little direct financial reward to be gained from building show gardens. Semken Landscaping are often co-sponsors, so they have to absorb their own labour, equipment and administration costs. Show gardens are very much morale-building exercises. 'That really is important. Our people queue up to work on the show gardens. It's one of the few times that we would have 20 people working together—not necessarily on the same site—but in the same area. They love that. They love working in a big group, because normally they go in twos and threes. So to have them all working together, they think that's fun. They are putting their skills on show.'

Mark also appreciates the prestige value of the work. 'It's the contacts we've made in the industry that are important. We're showcasing our company to the public, but mainly we're showcasing our company to the rest of the industry. Maybe we're creating a myth that we're the company that can do anything. But the motivation behind building the best show garden you can, is to showcase and promote your company. To do that, you must go into every show garden determined to build a gold-medal show garden. You'll always go in to win gold.'

chapter five

A moment of inspiration

THE GARDEN THAT was to travel to Chelsea began its life as a joint venture at the 2003 Melbourne International Flower and Garden Show. The year before, Jim Fogarty had designed and built a gold-medal winning garden with the help of a landscaper, and through a partnership with Larkman Nurseries, a plant propagator. This was Jim's first gold medal and this garden was also awarded the Royal Horticultural Society of Victoria's Comeadow Award for Design Excellence. This was the garden Jim had to finish himself, the garden where he had refused the help of Martin and Mark of Semken Landscaping. Since that time, Jim had connected with Semken Landscaping—they were building some of his gardens; so the 2003 garden was to be a joint venture, jointly owned by Larkman Nurseries, Semken Landscaping and Jim Fogarty Design. 'I'd commit my design and creative management for free, Semken

Landscaping would build it for free,' and Larkman would provide the plants, cover the cost of the consumables and provide certain other services. Most importantly, Jim maintained artistic control.

The partnership was sealed with a handshake at a meeting in late 2002. But by this time—because MIFGS is held in April each year—Jim's design was well underway. Even before the 2002 show was finished Jim remembers, 'I had in my head this idea of a firewood wall. I believe that people go to the show to get ideas. I think people also like to see new ideas for walls: a little quirky, perhaps theatrical. I guess the idea stems back to how, when I first left school, I cut firewood for two years. I had also just read a book called *Jackson's Track*, about a woodcutter and set in Gippsland.

'I don't know what it is, whether it's the smell of the wood split open—that fresh, bush smell—or even just the feeling of a beautiful log; there's something quite romantic and stimulating about it. It goes right back to the old pioneering days, and it's quite a "blokey" thing: using the axe, chopping wood, working outdoors. There's a lot of things that evoke a lot of good emotions for me. At the end of the day, when you've stacked up the firewood, it's a very homely feeling. You picture the roast dinner and the hot bread coming out of the oven.

'Stacked firewood, done well, looks terrific, and I began to believe there was something in it for a show garden. That's the beginning, although it sat in my head for weeks before I put anything down on paper.' In fact the first sketch plan of the firewood wall is dated July 21, 2002 and shows the firewood erected on top of a retaining wall clad with 'crazy sawn bluestone' and with redgum sleeper capping; three ideas that were to re-emerge in rather different forms in the evolution of the design.

Jim does not begin with 'themes' or 'topics' for his show gardens.

Had he decided at this early point that his next garden would follow an 'Australian' theme, the end result would probably have been quite different, and far less original. Think Australian, think native plants; that would be the usual, clichéd design path most would have followed. But Jim began with a feeling, not a theme; a feeling he could touch and smell: sawn log ends clad with smooth and rough bark which would became a wall, a feature, a focal point. But not just any old wall. This was to be a wall that emerged from his own life experience, a wall that would symbolise 'Australia' in a much more subtle, meaningful and original way. It was to prove an inspired moment.

The firewood all came from Larkman Nurseries, cut from fallen branches or dead trees, all eucalyptus. Jim is quite adamant about this and was deeply offended when one 'smart-arse' observer asked him, 'How many trees died so this wall could be built?' 'The fact is, if the wood's too green it's not going to look right for what we want, so all the wood had to come from dead branches or dead trees. Geoff Martin from the nursery cut it all with a chainsaw. I think there were something like 15 trailer loads all up, quite a bit of firewood.'

The unusual, natural look of the firewood was beginning to suggest a pattern. 'I went to a dinner party and I met this guy, Rick Lindsay, from Mansfield (in the High Country, north-east of Melbourne). Rick was a typically Australian country bloke—lovely guy, very funny and laconic and a bit of a larrikin.' Jim would not have been taking in much of the dinner party. He would have been smiling charmingly and making pleasant, friendly small talk, because that's the sort of bloke he is. But his head would have been full of his firewood wall. He asked Rick what he did for a living, as you do. Then suddenly Jim's eyes and mind focused: Rick built walls! Not just any old walls; he built rammed earth walls. 'I felt

I had a lot in common with him. I had no knowledge what rammed earth walls were then; I was quite intrigued. Perhaps I was thinking, even then, there could be something in this; these rammed earth walls sound quite interesting: rammed earth walls and firewood, I imagined they could go hand in hand.'

Rick sent Jim to several locations where he could see rammed earth walls in situ. He went to a place in Frankston and to a winery at Main Ridge, both on the Mornington Peninsular, not far out of Melbourne. He also sent him to Lauriston Girls' School: 'He'd done a big wall of it there. I was really quite impressed.' Jim had seen a number of mudbrick houses, with separately moulded large mud bricks laid in courses to make a roughly built wall, then covered with a cement slurry. 'But the rammed earth wasn't really like that. It was very finished and very architectural and very clean-looking: well-built, but it still had that really earthy, gutsy, blokey feel to it— purely because of its colour and texture. A very bony texture, because they literally ram the layers of earth inside a formwork and you get that strata look. And if parts of it aren't rammed overly, you get a really bony texture to it. Aggregate. Like on a riverbank; a compressed, compacted clay look. You might chip a bit of it off and you can see a bit of the aggregate in there, and grit. So I thought it looked fantastic, really.' Jim believes this material has a lot of depth of character: 'It wasn't just concrete and I like the idea there was a bit of a story behind it, and you could picture the blokes making it and ramming it; it's quite labour intensive.' And like the firewood wall, this material is only one step away from the bush, from the natural earth.

The next element Jim had to find was the pavers. If a theme was beginning to emerge it was a hand-made, rough-sawn look. Quite a lot of pavers would be needed: surrounding the garden, between the walls and the lawn, and flooring the open-air lounge room area. The colours of the walls—firewood and rammed earth—moved from pale cream through yellow to pinkish red. Jim needed a cool, darker colour tone for contrast. Charcoal, or perhaps a deep metallic blue. He settled for a range of 'bluestone' shades. The original thought of facing the retaining walls with bluestone had been abandoned once the lovely tones of the rammed earth had been discovered. Bluestone is probably historic Melbourne's most ubiquitous building material. Plains to the west of Melbourne, running for several hundred kilometres into the Western District, are full of volcanic basalt. Great quarries were opened up so the stratas of stone could be mined for city buildings and laid down for roads and laneways. The pervading colour of old Melbourne is the blue-grey of this bluestone. Even a few modern buildings, such as the National Gallery of Victoria, are built of bluestone dug from these quarries.

Jim wanted a bluestone-coloured paver, and luckily he knew a man who made pavers to order: Mick Hoban of Cast In Stone. Mick wasn't making them from actual bluestone; he was using coloured cement. But Jim wanted a reddish fleck through it, as happens with the natural bluestone. 'I wanted this iron look.' Mick showed Jim a product he was developing, using recycled brown glass blended through the cement: 'Two millimetre bits of broken beer bottles. So Mick made me a sample of this paver with the exposed beer bottle glass in it and a bluestone cement background. It looked stunning. It looked like little bits of rusted iron filing. Earthy again, and it played with the colour scheme of the firewood and the rammed earth.' And 'blokey' enough, even for Jim!

But Mick couldn't locate enough of the glass for the number of pavers Jim needed, 'So we had to come up with another solution. Following up for a *Backyard Blitz* design I'd gone down to this quarry at Arthur's Seat in Dromana on the Mornington Peninsular:

Hill View Quarries. The business was left to charity by the bloke who founded it and everyone loves their job down there because all the profits go to charity. Since it's an open cut granite quarry the guy took me down into the bottom of it. It was a Friday afternoon and it was drizzling rain. It was a really moody atmosphere: dark clouds and there was a bit of a storm brewing. You've got these 60-metre high, sheer granite rock-faces, with roadways coming down for the big trucks. They'd explode a wall and you'd get all this rubble cascading down. It was like being on another planet.' Jim took Mick some samples of the granite and a fragment of one of Rick's rammed earth pieces, to get the colour scheme right. 'Granite often has iron in it, which has a reddish, earthy tinge to it. So Mick at Cast In Stone did another sample using crushed granite and exposed it so you see the actual granite aggregate through the top of the paver. He did a bull-nose capping as well, which is what you put on top of the wall. Jim wanted to break up the paving a little more, so he impregnated river pebbles, also from Mansfield, into a concrete slurry. 'They came originally from a mudrock, so the colours are chocolatey and very striking.' The pavers looked really good and I couldn't be happier. Mick was really happy with them too and he made all the pavers for free.'

With show gardens you often have a dozen or more companies involved all supplying their own product; gratis. It might just be the pots or the furniture, but each of these minor sponsors receives an acknowledgment on signage at the front of the garden, and the thousands of visitors who pass the exhibit during the show can note where the various items can be obtained.

Jim was anxious that the sightlines for his garden should be available from as many positions as possible. The firewood wall enclosed the rear, 'outdoor room' area of the garden on three sides only. The rammed earth retaining walls, only approximately 700 millimetres high as seen from the viewing platforms, did not obstruct vision at all. To ensure vision from either sides of the garden, walls of rusted, open reinforcing mesh were specified, so you could 'see into the garden and psychologically "enter" the garden. So it became three-dimensional, not just existing on one plane, which is how it would have seemed, viewed only from the front.' A jarrah decking viewing platform was designed, encompassing the garden along the front and the two sides. This further enhanced vision. Visitors could stand right up against the open rusted mesh and the mesh seemed to disappear, giving an uninterrupted view of the garden and all its details. Building on that and breaking the monotony of the rammed earth retaining walls, Jim introduced several panels of Mini Orb. 'Which is a modern version of the old corrugated iron, but it doesn't rust.' The furniture was all obtained from Matt Heritage Design from Bendigo, an old 'gold rush' provincial city in central Victoria. 'He had this curved garden bench, he called "Duckboard" made out of jarrah, an Australian hardwood, with a steel frame.' Later in the year Jim took a trip to Asia to a friend's wedding. 'I was in a nightclub in Bangkok. The roof seemed quite low. It was like being in a ship. I thought that there was something quite cosy about this, and that was the inspiration behind the lounge area, with the cushions.'

Although the garden developed principally in Jim's imagination, by late July he was beginning to jot down rough sketch plans. But still the mental process continued. 'I imagine I'm a 360 degree eyeball floating through a garden, able to look at things from all different angles, and I get a feeling if something's going to look good, or how to make it better. I might think about an area for several days, it might even bother me for three months, and then something will click and I'll come up with an idea. It evolves gradually.' The water feature for this garden eluded Jim for months. 'I struggled with the water feature and didn't get it right until the end. I wanted to come up with something that was unique, but I wanted it to be simple and to suit everything else.' He certainly didn't want anything even vaguely resembling a classical fountain. 'This was the time of the "Tuscan garden" being very fashionable. I'd been to Tuscany and I was questioning why we were copying Tuscan gardens and why we weren't developing our own Australian feel for our gardens. Why couldn't Australia have its own style?' That was developing as the basis for the overall design intent, but it had to be sophisticated and contemporary. Not a rustic bush garden with concrete kookaburras, old wagon wheels and furniture made from twisted tea-tree trunks. 'I always wanted it to be quite architectural and "designed". That's why in the firewood wall I used the upright timber detailing which we painted a graphite colour, computer-matched off the pavers, because I didn't just want it to be just a stack of firewood. I didn't want it to be thrown together, and on-site we used stonemasons to build it.'

Finally, almost at the last moment, the idea for the water feature came quite quickly. Suddenly Jim thought of a 'pyramid stack' and that became the design. 'Originally I was playing around with sandstone. Then I went to the stone yard and I saw this black stone. I thought that that stone looked fantastic.' It was a black slate, cut into sheets 20mm thick. 'It's quite chunky and clean. It had a bit of strata and texture running through it and I had it cut into eight square pieces, from 80cm by 80cm with each piece reducing by 10cm square down to the smallest at 10cm square.' The water feature was built by Geoff Martin at Larkman Nurseries. I told him I wanted a pyramid with water running down it, and he did a great job building it. He's a jack of all trades—a welder, a fitter and turner—whatever you wanted. The water comes up through a hole in the middle of the pyramid and just runs down the other pieces,' from the smallest down to the largest and into a pond. 'Then came the pots. I just thought that the pots had to be rusted metal pots. They came out of a junkyard and were cut up into varying sizes, so they were cheap and easy to do. We sanded back some redgum sleepers and oiled them up and they became a nice little feature in the lawn. All the jarrah and redgum was recycled timber supplied by Peter Barnard. All he does is recycle timber and he loves his timber. He loves it so much he won't sell it! And there had to be a barbecue. I wanted this garden to be something people would look at and envisage in their own backyards. The barbecue was all stainless steel. I wanted that. I didn't want it looking rusty. I wanted it to look architectural and quite flash, a piece of good industrial design, sophisticated.' Jim chose the barbecue off a showroom floor and got it on loan. 'They had one there that wasn't too big or outrageous, just simple stainless steel with a hood. On-site we took the wheels off and simplified it a bit more.'

Somewhat perversely, if the 'built' features of the garden were emerging as genuinely Australian—albeit with a modern, sophisticated feel to them—the plants were to be exclusively exotics. 'Obviously, the choice of plants was based on a selection of the plants Larkman Nurseries grows. So it was just a matter of looking at his plant list.' The previous year, working with the same nurseryman, Jim used a lot of English perennial flowering plants, 'So at MIFGS, for this one, I was keen to do something different, use more foliage plants, more plants that thrived in the shade, like Plantain Lily (*Hostas* sp.) and *Arthropodium,* Alum Root (*Heucheras* sp.), *Heucherallas* and Kaffir Lily (*Clivia* sp.).' The woodstack and rammed earth walls, the pavers and the black stone water feature provided the textures and colours. 'The plants were only really there to soften the whole thing and bring the green right back into it. They were all grown from about eight months prior to the show. There's no flowering plants as such, only the Kaffir Lily. There's one plant that the nurseryman was really keen to put in. I was probably a bit gutless because I let it happen. Probably one of the only regrets I've got about that garden is that I did put it in, because I never believed that it suited the garden, but I allowed three little pots, that was all.' The offending plant was *Nemesia* 'Vanilla Mist'. 'It had a beautiful perfume. Great plant—it just didn't really suit the garden. I did it because he was promoting his plants. But I wouldn't do it if I had my time again. There were also a lot of succulents in pots, and there was also the lawn. There was a lot of hard surfacing in there, so I had to soften it with green stuff.'

The design specified three trees, virtually identical, to be placed in the two front corners and one near the rear, on the left. 'I went to Fleming's Nurseries for the trees. I went up to Taggerty, to one of their big growing yards up there, as they were lending me the trees. They had this Chinese Elm (*Ulmus parvifolia*) and the variety was "Churchyard". Now there's a tree outside St John's Church in Toorak Road.' This church is a beautiful stone structure built in the 1800s, and Jim's family has attended this church for several generations. Jim travelled by tram past this church every school day on his way to Melbourne Grammar, right past the glorious Chinese Elm out the front. 'At that age I wouldn't have noticed it, but I see it a lot now. It's a beautiful tree, and the "habit", or shape of it, is just uniform and quite amazing to look at. This variety that Fleming's were growing came from a cutting off this parent tree. So they're all exact clones off that exact tree, which is why they call it "Churchyard". My grandmother's ashes are in the garden at that churchyard, so I picked and tagged three out of a row of 200 of these things, all from the same tree. From most people's point of view it would be hard to tell the difference. It was midwinter and they had no leaves on them. All I was looking for was the right shape of the branching of the canopy, so in the show garden they'd provide the perfect shape for the space selected; the other corner would be taken up by the water feature.' So he knew the planting scheme had to be shade-loving with these big trees dominating; trees which would still be in green leaf by the time of MIFGS in April. So even though, in reality, any sort of plant would have survived in the shade for a week, Jim knew that 'horticultural reality' demanded plants for a shady area.

In Melbourne, you are allowed nine days to build a show garden. 'We go in on the Monday and at 2pm of the Tuesday of the following week is judging. The first day is your site set-out, so you peg out the site and where you'll lay pavers for the footings. Semken Landscaping supplied a basic team of four for the construction. There was also Geoff, the jack-of-all-trades from the nursery, and Simon, also from the nursery. The rammed earth walls were set in place quite early. They had been made in Mansfield and were transported down by truck, 'So they had to be picked up by a crane, loaded onto the truck, unloaded off the truck in Melbourne with a crane, then picked up with a forklift and positioned on-site.' Rick Lindsay had placed threaded reinforcing bars through the walls, which came out at the top, above the wall sections. He made a steel jib that fitted over the ends of these bars and the jib had a 'handle', a steel bar, so the crane could pick it up. 'At the Melbourne end he modified it, so forklift teeth could go through and pick them up. They were never seen in the garden, because once the sections were in place and mortared down, we ground off the tops of the bars and then we bull-nosed the top.' There were 15 rammed earth sections in all. 'Putting in the rammed earth walls took a full day. We couldn't help being a bit nervous about them cracking or breaking, because as the forklift was moving they'd swing. They were heavy, about three-quarters of a tonne each. That was probably the most stressful part of the building of the garden, getting in those rammed earth walls.

'You've got to remember that at Melbourne you can't excavate.' The whole area is a flourishing public park: Carlton Gardens. 'You can't dig down, so you can't plant plants into the ground, you've got to build up a "false ground", as they call it.' Which was why the design for Melbourne specified raised garden beds. 'So that a tree can go in—a tree bag is 60cm tall, and you need to put a shrub above that—so you're looking at something like 80cm above true ground level, which then has to be all filled up. So when the site's set out and the rammed earth walls are in, Geoff begins framing up for the fire-wood wall. The bull-nose capping went on the rammed earth walls and the paving had to be done, all the timberwork for pergolas and the mesh walls and all the fitting out. The Mini Orb and garden lighting went in. The trees were planted quite early, because they're heavy. They weigh a few hundred kilos each and they go in by hand, then they get built around.'

Meanwhile, the firewood wall was being built by Semken Landscaping's two stonemasons, Brad Peeters and Mark Stammers. 'They loved it. It was quite hot, all blue sky and sunny. I still remember them climbing up like monkeys, with their shirts off, and getting into stacking it up so that it was quite well done, not just thrown together.' They carefully selected each log, as though it was a piece of building stone, and fitted it into place. But unlike stone, the firewood couldn't be struck with a tool to chip off pieces until it was the right shape and size. Small logs had to be positioned between larger ones—'chinked'—so the spaces were filled as tightly as possible. As the log wall grew the effect became increasingly impressive, just as Jim had imagined it would. The random pattern of round log ends and the varying colours of the different eucalypt species—yellows and browns, pinks and reds—was enticingly attractive, almost mesmerising in its overall effect. 'You just start daydreaming about log fires and country kitchens and hot bread.' Martin Semken was in overall charge; Jim's was one of seven show gardens Semken Landscaping were building that year, but this was the first show garden that Martin and Jim had worked on together. 'Marty was fantastic. We certainly got to know each very well during that construction period, as you do when you work closely with someone. We forged a great friendship out of that, really.' Everyone worked long hours and they worked hard. 'It seems like a dozen guys were crawling over that site for nine days.

'While the Semken Landscaping guys are building it, my job is to stand back, because they're right in the garden and they're focusing on all the corners and all the little details—a millimetre or two here and a millimetre there. I try and stand back and look for faults.' Jim would even walk away and then come back to re-focus, to see it afresh. 'I look for faults. I'm the arsehole who comes up and changes something slightly, or says, "Look, you can see that join, when you stand back in the shadow. Is there any way we can patch that up a bit more?" That's fine, because they know I'm not criticising their workmanship, my job is to look for the faults so we can improve the standard. I'd never done a show garden with them before, and I've certainly got a lot of respect for them. As a team we all got on really well, had a lot of laughs. I think some of the guys—as the garden began to develop—I think they "got it". As the walls went in, someone from IMG—the show organisers—said they didn't understand what I was thinking. The scale changes from the first day and at first everything looks small. Once you start building out of the ground, it all looks big again.'

After the construction goes in, the hard phase is virtually finished. 'The hard phase probably takes about six days. There'd be an overlap at the weekend. On Saturday you'd probably start "prepping" for your soft phase and finishing off your hard phase. Mulch would be arriving, the plants would be arriving, you'll be watering the plants and it's a different mindset now, because you're not making mortar and there's no cement involved. So while the construction guys are finishing off, sponging and cleaning grout and things, I guess Marty Semken starts thinking about the soft phase, and my mind is now switching over to the planting phase, for while you can build a garden beautifully well, you can still stuff it up with the plants. If the plants are not good enough quality, it's not going to bring you from bronze or silver to gold.'

Then the planting went in. 'Very cleverly, Marty brings in a separate "soft team", who are more plant-based people. It freshens up the crew a bit. The construction crew have worked hard and they get a bit tired. Simon Dawson from Semken Landscaping came in, we had another Simon from Larkman Nurseries, and myself, and we gradually started at the back corner and worked our way out with the plants. Then the front and side decking went in. With 130-odd thousand people going past, I thought it would be a good idea to have a viewing platform. We were staining it up until midnight one night; the days are quite long but it all came together.' Finally it was Tuesday. 'That last day Bency was there helping with the clean-up and sweeping up around the grass. You're working right up until that last moment and it's quite tense and Marty is running on adrenalin and so am I. Two o'clock's judging and we worked right up until a quarter to two and then Marty and Bency finally said, "Right boys, tools in the ute. Done. Walk away from it." You need someone to tap you on the shoulder and say, "Right, mate. Forget about it now. It's in other people's hands from now on." It's hard to explain but it's almost surreal to see it finished, standing there in three dimensions. You've had it in your head for a year. It develops in your head. You've had the odd night where you dream of this garden and you wake up and—click! You've got the water feature. To see it finished is a very powerful experience. At that moment there were probably eight of us, and with the other Semken Landscaping crews from the other gardens we just walked down to the pub and had a few beers. It was a nine-day set-up, but for me it's been a year of living with this garden. Everyone just shuts down and you go into a sort of dumb mode, almost.'

No one connected with the garden is around when the judges come by. 'No, I don't want to be there.' Jim thinks it's unprofessional. He doesn't even know how many judges are involved. He thinks there could be as many as 18—six teams of three. Jim has worked as a show garden judge himself, in New Zealand. 'It was a good experience on the other side of the fence. Over there I worked in a group of three, with Julian Dowle from England and Koji Ninomiya from Japan. That was a great honour. I know Julian quite well now.' But Jim treasures his time with Koji: 'He's got an innate ability with plants. He understands the way to present plants; the Japanese way with show gardens. I remember there was one garden that had bamboo, and they'd planted the bamboo straight. But of course when you do that, because it's not rooted, overnight it criss-crosses itself. That doesn't happen in nature. But there's a trick. You tilt them slightly forward, so they lean forward, so when you look at them they look straight and they don't criss-cross.'

That night Jim received a phone call from IMG, telling him to be at the official breakfast in the morning. 'They wouldn't tell me why. They said it was a surprise.' Jim already knew that if you received that call the night before, you had almost certainly won a gold medal. 'So I thought that we must have won gold. So I rang Marty and said, "Mate, I've just had the phone call, so we must have done well. Congratulations!" Jim went to the breakfast 'all suited up' with Martin Semken and Clive Larkman. In the presence of Steve Bracks, Premier of Victoria; Mrs Landy, wife of Governor John Landy; and John So, Lord Mayor of Melbourne, they were presented with their gold medal. Jim had also won the Royal Victorian Horticultural Society's Design Excellence Award, the Comeadow Award. 'I won that the year before as well, so to get it two years in a row is really good. And then, totally surprisingly, we got the best in the show, the Lord Mayor's Award. It was quite humbling, to get all three. It just made me think that something special was happening in this friendship between Marty, Bency and I.'

Winning awards is all very well, but Jim gets his greatest pleasure from the public's reactions to his gardens. 'I love it when the show's open to the public. That's when you learn a lot. You're standing in the crowd like an ordinary punter, no one knows who you are, and you just stand there and listen to the comments. Not everyone is going to love it, you can't expect everyone to love it. I actually like that some don't like the garden, because if everyone liked it, then it probably wouldn't be all that exciting. It's in those first few seconds, when someone walks up, and it's that release of breath. You can literally hear them: "Aaah! Look, darling, come and have a look at this!" You're looking at them and they're not seeing what you see, all the faults. They're seeing the overall thing, and you realise that's what you've been trying to achieve, to give that overall pleasure to someone—an old lady or a young kid.'

Jim believes you owe it to your sponsors to give them as much media attention as you can. Gold medals help. Lots of picture opportunities are even better. 'The more photo opportunities you can provide in a garden that are totally different from the other photo opportunities, the more print exposure you're going to get. A magazine might get six different shots out of one garden. It's all about zooming in. You should be able to zoom into any corner of a garden and get a front cover for a magazine. In fact the *Daily Telegraph* in London, early in February 2004, ran a big colour close-up of the water feature in their gardening section: the black stone pyramid.' Geoff Martin from Larkman Nurseries, who built it, would never have guessed in a million years that his work would feature in one of Britain's most prestigious newspapers. But he had built it well enough, and there it was. 'How many Poms would see that? About four million?'

Jim has no regrets when a show garden is pulled down at the end of the week. The plants, furniture and fittings are returned to their rightful owners and the rest—mainly rubble—is trucked out. 'Doesn't worry me. From the beginning you know it's a show garden, so you've got to build it in such a way that it can be pulled down. But you can't help being attached to it; you can't help feeling some regret that you will never see that garden again. At the time I would never have thought in a million years that we'd see the garden again. But the Chelsea garden is quite different. There are some similarities and some of it is exactly the same, but because the timing's different, the garden's different and it's really been cranked up and improved. Since we built the Melbourne one, we all know the Semken Landscaping boys will push the quality even further. Melbourne was very good. Chelsea will be, hopefully, even better.'

chapter six

The green ceiling

WES FLEMING DID not bring skills as a garden designer or land-scaper to the *Australian Inspiration* syndicate. He brought passion, enthusiasm and a commitment to the 'bigger picture'. Very early in the discussions Wes Fleming's firm, Fleming's Nurseries, agreed to finance the project in its exploratory stage. They also agreed to financially underwrite the entire venture if necessary, to see it through to its—hopefully—triumphant end. At first Wes believed this would be seeding money, enough to get the idea underway and attract sponsorship from large corporations. The team worked hard to achieve solid sponsorship from airlines and others, but their efforts were in vain, although some support has come from horticul-tural suppliers and the Melbourne International Flower and Garden Show. But the level of Fleming's commitment meant that the garden became known officially as *Fleming's Nurseries 'Australian Inspiration'*.

Fleming's main nursery occupies 150 acres of beautiful rolling country at Monbulk, on the edge of the Dandenong Ranges—that spur of the Great Dividing Range that comes closest to Melbourne. The family has amassed a further 3000 acres in the Yarra Valley and at Taggerty. The original nursery was established by Wes's grandfather, Eric Fleming, who worked for the Nobelius Nursery, an organisation so extensive they had their own siding on the narrow gauge railway that still winds its way through those beautiful hills. Among a wide range of horticultural products, Nobelius had been selling fruit tree rootstock to the orchard industry since early in the 20th century. Eric Fleming began growing rootstock for Nobelius Nursery and when Nobelius finally went out of business during the 1920s, Eric expanded his operation and continued to grow rootstock and finished trees on a few acres in Monbulk. The climate in the Dandenong Ranges is temperate, with a high rainfall and a deep volcanic soil that makes it ideal country for nurserymen and berry growers. Eric Fleming had six sons and five daughters, and they provided a ready—if not always willing—labour source for his nursery during the long, desperate years of the Depression and through into World War II. They were hard times. The Flemings lived largely off the land, trapping rabbits and growing vegetables and working from dawn to dusk. 'My father Don had limited schooling, missing it much of the time when there was work to be done on the farm, and leaving when he was about 13 years of age. The Fleming kids all went to Macclesfield State School.' Up to Don's time it was the family's sole source of formal education: 'We call it "Macclesfield University". There were only about 13 children at the school, and most of them were Flemings. It was a funny little school, and Dad apparently only went to Grade 4 or Grade 5.'

Following the death of Eric Fleming, Wes's father Don and his five brothers took over the nursery and it grew steadily through the post-war years. 'After 30 years, through natural attrition, the partnership came down to three brothers, then in the early 1980s Mum and Dad bought the business from my uncles.' Wes, his brother, his father and his mother now run the company, which has moved into the fourth generation: 'Traditionally we are known as a fruit tree nursery and our biggest market was into the commercial orchard industry. Midway through the second generation we started to expand into ornamentals, predominantly flowering fruit trees. So you'd have flowering prunus, flowering apricots, flowering peaches, flowering cherries. It was a natural progression from growing fruit trees to growing flowering fruit trees.' This period coincided with a time during which flowering fruit trees were being favoured by municipal councils for street plantings. This boom in ornamental exotics meant big business for Fleming's Nurseries. 'When the third generation came into the company we had a fairly solid background in ornamentals, but not a big range.' By then, approximately half the nursery's sales would have been wholesaling to retail nurseries, the other half to orchardists.

As one of the directors of the company Wes took a great interest in the ornamentals. The homesick, earliest European settlers in the Dandenong Ranges planted the trees from their native lands, and now these hills are beautiful with magnificent stands of exotic trees, especially during the autumn. Since 1983, when Wes's immediate family took over the company, 'We've had a huge expansion in size.' Wes claims Fleming's Nurseries is the biggest open ground nursery in the country. 'We have the potential for considerable expansion if we manage the whole process well.' A lot of the company's recent expansion has been in serving the orchard industry; but in a specific direction. 'We like to pretend we're clever, but probably it was more hard work than anything else, and a dedication to doing the job.' The company began handling international fruit breeders' products and pioneering the importation of protected cultivars into the country. The new and improved cultivars changed the direction of the fruit industry in Australia by allowing orchardists to compete on the world market. Australia was no longer behind the rest of the world with up-to-date cultivars. 'As a result, the orchard side of the business expanded four or five-fold in a matter of—probably—less than a decade.' But Fleming's were still thinking ahead: 'With the orchard industry going along nicely we turned our focus to the retail garden centres and the ornamental side of the business, to try and plan ahead for the plateauing or decline in our orchard sales. We scoured the world looking for new and exciting ornamentals, and we have introduced many new cultivars into the market.' Fleming's are nationwide, dealing all over Australia. 'We're not a company that just sits and rides out the good times, we're working hard against the bad times coming. This recent time of drought has been a trying time for our customers around Australia; water-related issues are a limiting factor, but we are working through these negatives towards a positive future.'

Wes believes another boom time for native plants is coming, but not to the home garden market. 'It was very much a home-garden driven market a decade ago. I think this is going to be more on the municipal side of things: street trees, parks and so on, but we do need careful selection.' Wes has little time for the native-only fanatics. 'Understand that I've got a bent towards exotics, but there's a lot of flawed logic being used at the moment.' Fire is a major concern. 'Most exotics are natural fire buffers, but what we're really about is the right tree in the right position, and sometimes no tree is the right tree, sometimes an exotic is the right tree. It depends. Next bushfire season, if we have had bad bushfires, people won't want natives near their properties. But I believe everyone should be encouraged to plant trees and I don't care what sort of trees they are. It's good for the environment.' Which brings us very close to the source of Wes's passion and to one of the principal reasons why he's supported *Australian Inspiration* so wholeheartedly, and at such financial cost.

Each year, trees in our large cities are becoming fewer and fewer. The urban green canopy is diminishing. Look out of the aircraft window as you fly into any Australian city today, and you will see that the tree cover is thinning; the oases are disappearing; the green cover is vanishing. There is a lot of 'green interest' in Australia, but trees are not being planted. 'If you go through any housing developments being built—and this goes for nearly all of Australia during recent times—you'll be lucky to see a tree over the roofline. The only tall trees you'll see are the ones the developers were not allowed to remove in the first place. The trend in the home garden is for smaller trees. We deal in that market—people don't want the big trees. When I was growing up, the traditional suburban building block was a quarter of an acre. There are developments around now where the block size is a tenth of an acre.' Houses are getting bigger and more of them are being pushed into smaller and smaller areas of land, leaving little or no room for trees. 'We're becoming a litigious society. We worry about planting trees in our backyard because they might upset the neighbours. The roots might damage his swimming pool, so he's going to sue me. Stories abound about tree roots breaking down foundations, so people aren't planting trees, they're planting shrubs.' Parklands are shrinking as the land is overtaken by sports stadiums, car parks, freeways and educational institutions.

Wes Fleming believes we're going to have a shortage of trees in our built environment in the next 20 years. 'All trees have got a lifespan. If we're not replacing the ones that are dying, we're going to have a net loss. But what a lot of people don't understand is how important trees are to us; and not just for their aesthetics. A typical four-cylinder car built after 1987 and driven 20,000 kilometres a year produces five tonnes of greenhouse gases. Just to convert the carbon monoxide back to oxygen takes the respiration of 500 mature trees per car. A well-positioned tree in a domestic landscape can reduce heating and cooling costs in a building by up to 20 per cent. So the more trees we use in our landscape the healthier our environment will be. I might be a nurseryman telling this story, but it's obviously so simple: the best way we can all go green is to plant more trees.' We also need to plan more open space. 'You can see estates around now that really plan their tree usage very well—and their public open space—but the slums of tomorrow are still being built,' often with the barest suggestion of gardens; plants choking between high brick walls, cramped, blocked from sunlight and ulti-mately unsustainable.

Wes worries about the inner urban areas, where town houses and high-rise apartment blocks are being built over former domestic gar-dens and other treed areas. 'I think we need to look at our urban environment, to look at canopy coverage and to plan for best-case scenarios, long-term.' The apparent divide between the conserva-tion movement and the horticultural industry disturbs him. 'We're at opposite ends of the spectrum. Our company, we grow exotics, so we're the archenemy of the conservation movement. Yet I believe we're on the same team. We should be a lot closer together, fighting the big concrete monsters rather than each other.' He sees an example of how things should be, with the farming lobby and the environmentalists coming together to deal with salinity. Wes believes that the urban canopy can only be saved and restored through a series of laws, but changes in legislation can only come through public pressure, which follows on from public education.

Wes believes garden shows can be a prime force in the education of the public: garden shows can elevate the status of growing things—in a community and in a nation. 'I think we in the horticultural industry haven't worked out how best to use garden shows. The garden shows in Melbourne are still based around shit and glitter. Still based around a disposable garden and what looks good.' Fleming's took a decision six or seven years ago to 'Put our money where our mouth is, to support the garden show and perhaps encourage other horticultural firms to come on board and promote our industry.' There was no direct financial benefit to be gained; they sell nothing at the shows, which do not really cater for their customers: orchardists and wholesale tree buyers. Fleming's believed they could lift the profile of horticulturists and the status of the Melbourne International Flower and Garden Show by introducing a series of student design competitions. 'We run the Don Fleming International Student Design competition, named in honour of my father. All entrants are students of horticulture and garden design. We give them a brief to design to and a budget under which to work. We select four finalists, one New Zealander and three Australians, and we construct their gardens at MIFGS. A panel of judges selects the overall winner, who receives a trip for two to the Chelsea Flower Show, with spending money and a cash component. The reason we started it was to raise the profile of horticulture in general.'

Wes is a nurseryman without formal qualifications. 'I'm without a piece of paper, but I have the advantage of having played in the dirt. I learned the trade from the ground up.' He grew tired of going to functions 'and talking to people—at parties and events—and they'd come up and you'd start some chit-chat going, and they'd ask you what you did. You'd tell them you're a nurseryman and their eyes would glaze over, they'd look over your shoulder and around the room and go and find somebody more interesting to talk to. Horticulture was not seen as a professional industry or a worthwhile career. I believe teachers recommended horticulture as a last resort.' So Fleming's perceived their student competition, and the Melbourne garden show itself, as an important way to raise public awareness of horticulture as a worthwhile profession. The winner of the 2002 student design award 'went on to win the national student of the year award, across all disciplines of education. One of the main points in her resume was that she had won the Don Fleming student award. So we were pretty chuffed about that! We know that other finalists have landed jobs or good career moves through their success in these awards.'

Wes believes the Australian horticultural industry is not thinking on a large enough scale. He compares it to the situation in Britain. Wimbledon and the Chelsea Flower Show are London's two biggest events. Chelsea launches the London 'season'. Each night of the show, BBC TWO broadcasts a one-hour telecast, between eight and nine, right across southern England. The programs, presented by nationally known personalities, broadcast live links from Chelsea: pre-filmed, on-location background stories about many of the show gardens and other exhibits; and interviews with garden designers and gardeners, and everyday visitors to the show. Some of the background stories are even filmed overseas. The programs are expertly produced, using the latest digital effects and techniques, and all done with a great sense of pride in gardening and in gardeners, professional and amateur. The overall impression is of real excitement, vivid colour, outstanding design, fascinating detail, and a proliferation of gardening hints and advice. Riveting viewing for anyone even vaguely interested in gardening, and, more importantly, many who may not be, yet. And because it is the BBC, the programs are totally non-commercial, with not a single advertisement in sight. But what a magnificent 'advertisement' they are for the British horticultural industry.

Contrast this with the television coverage accorded the Melbourne International Flower and Garden Show. Apart from the relatively short segments on such national gardening programs as *Burke's Backyard* and the ABC's *Gardening Australia,* Wes dares to dream of the ABC emulating the BBC's example and running a well-produced, non-commercial nightly program through the week of the garden show. He believes it would create enormous interest and attract substantial corporate backing for MIFGS. This contrast between the BBC's effort and the coverage of the Melbourne show epitomises Wes's belief in a need to internationalise the Australian horticulture industry. 'This is the overwhelming reason why I have helped to take the garden to the Chelsea Flower Show. To show the world that we have designers, landscapers and nurseries that are equal to the best. One ex-pat Australian came up to me at Chelsea and said, "I was so excited when I heard an Aussie garden was coming to Chelsea this year. I know we are as good as they are. Now you have proved it."

'The potential for Fleming's Nurseries to export into the

European market is quite high. It's an avenue that we've never explored, but with the development of our company, and the overseas markets we'll be looking at, it's not going to hurt us to get out there. We do have a product we can sell internationally.' Wes also knows that if Australian endeavour is to be recognised and acclaimed at home, it usually has to win accolades overseas. It's the old Australian cultural cringe, and success out in the 'big world' almost inevitably guarantees adulation back home. Every day, Australian newspapers are full of these stories: our actors and film directors at the Academy Awards, our cricketers in India, our athletes at the Olympic Games, our novelists at the Booker Prize; and hopefully, our show gardens at the Chelsea Flower Show.

Wes still can't believe how the *Australian Inspiration* project got started: 'It is amazing.' It happened at the 2003 Melbourne International Flower and Garden Show at which Jim Fogarty's garden—the basis for the Chelsea Australian garden—won several awards, including best in the show. As well as sponsoring the student design competition, Fleming's were one of the sponsors of the Collingwood Football Club. As a cross-promotion, Wes had arranged for Collingwood footballers to visit the garden show, meet show patrons, sign autographs and have lunch in one of the winning student gardens. It was Sunday, and at 'about 10am we got word that none of the footballers were able to come. We already had people standing around in their Collingwood garb waiting for the footballers to turn up, so I had to go down and pull the pin. But I still had the chef, I had the food, I had drink; I had everything, but nobody to sit in there and come to lunch. So there I was, standing there at about 10.30, thinking in good horticultural-speak: "Shit! What am I going to do?"'

Through the crowd Wes saw four people approaching: 'Jim Fogarty, who had already come to one of our luncheons, and Martin Semken, Mark Bence and Andrew Triantafillou, all from Semken Landscaping. So I went out and asked, "Do you guys want to come and have lunch?" Great!' So at the prearranged time of 11am they all turned up and sat down to lunch. Jim had designed the multi-award winning show garden and Semken Landscaping had built it. 'They were all on a high. The winners had been announced back on the Wednesday, but they were still all on a high. Somebody asked, "What's our next challenge?" Then somebody else said—no one can remember exactly who it was—but somebody actually said, "Why don't we take this garden to the Chelsea Flower Show?"' No one had had very much to drink, the lunch hadn't progressed very far, and Wes realised everyone was serious. Perhaps he saw the potential at this point, who knows? Perhaps he saw this as a chance to put Australian horticulture on the world map. Perhaps he realised that this foray onto the international stage would echo back in Australia, lifting the status of MIFGS and of the whole industry. Anyway, it might have been a wild dream at this point, but he took them seriously. 'I got on the phone to Greg Hooton of the International Management Group, who are the event organisers of MIFGS. I said, "Greg, I've got Bency, Marty, Jim and Drewy down here having lunch, and we're going to the Chelsea Flower Show. We think you'd better come down and talk to us." So Greg came down and sat with us over lunch, talking about the Chelsea Flower Show. Talking about how hard it was, actually. Trying to put a dampener, put the kibosh on it. Telling us it was pie in the sky stuff.' But Greg Hooton saw the others were determined, so then he began telling them in practical terms how they should go about it, the steps they needed to take to turn their wild dream into reality.

'And within three weeks, Jim, Martin, Mark and I were in London, at the Chelsea Flower Show, doing a reconnaissance trip. I hadn't been to the Chelsea Flower Show before. The week of the show falls in our busiest fortnight of the year. It's the start of our season—our winter season. Our deliveries Australia-wide begin on June 1, so the last 10 days in May are just absolute bedlam. It's all hands on deck. We work seven long days a week.' But Wes finally got there. Before he went he wrote an article for a trade magazine, talking about the myth, the aura of Chelsea, the gardening Olympics. Would the myth hold up? Wes believes it did. 'Some of the gardens there had the equivalent of a million Australian dollars spent on them,' so the competition would be fierce. 'I believed that if any Australian contingent was going to do well at Chelsea, we would be the one. I was 100 per cent confident in the design, I was 140 per cent confident in the construction. My belief in Semken Landscaping is without question. But I was a bit nervous about the plants. They had to be sourced in England and our people were not supervising their growth. However, our company has excellent nursery contacts in England and I felt confident the plants would be first-class. I was also worried about us—being Australian—displaying at Chelsea for the first time. But I felt that if we didn't win gold, or if we didn't even get a medal, I did believe we deserved to be there.'

chapter seven

Innocents abroad

THE THREE WEEKS that followed the end of the 2003 Melbourne International Flower and Garden Show was a frantic time for the four who were to become the *Australian Inspiration* team. For a few wild moments Jim, Wes, Martin and Mark believed they could somehow salvage the prize-winning Melbourne garden and then transport it across to London for the 2003 Chelsea Flower Show, scheduled for the last week in May. Greg Hooton of IMG, organisers of MIFGS, soon disabused them, telling them they would have to apply to the Royal Horticultural Society for a show garden space many months in advance; and that their chances were far from good. More than 150 show garden inquiries were received by the RHS, followed by more than 80 formal applications for fewer than 25 sites. He also told them that there had never been an Australian garden at Chelsea. Several had been attempted, but no one had succeeded. There had been international gardens at Chelsea from the USA,

Canada, Japan, South Africa, at least one of the Arab states, but there had never been an entry from Australia. This fact only made the team more determined than ever and, despite the odds, they resolved to fully investigate all the steps necessary to bring their garden to the Chelsea Flower Show in May 2004.

The day following that historic lunch Martin's wife, Anne Semken, began making phone calls. She called the British Consulate in Melbourne, the quarantine people to check the regulations both ways, and found the Royal Horticultural Society and Chelsea Flower Show websites on the Internet. It was very early days but Mark knew they would have to have some idea of what this whole ambitious project was going to cost, and so he prepared a notional budget. So far that preliminary costing has held up: 'It's been close. We've cut things out and we've chopped and changed, but the bottom line figure has never varied too far.' It has always been a realistic budget based on what they would have to spend, rather than what they could afford. 'We've economised where we can because funds are tight, but it was always about what we had to do to get the garden right.' They found out how early they would have to have every-thing ready to get it to London in time for the commencement of 'build-up' at Chelsea—allowing for all the delays that could occur moving the materials for an entire garden across the world by sea. As administration manager, Mark was already drawing up a schedule and creating the protocols that would carry them through that long year of preparation: 'All the basic principles that we've carried through were formulated in that first week.'

Right from the beginning they were all determined that the Chelsea garden would be built by a Semken Landscaping crew, flown in from Australia. They understood that the international gardens at Chelsea were usually built by British contractors, but the

Australian Inspiration team were determined that their garden would be built by their own people. The Semken Landscaping crews had an outstanding reputation for building award-winning gardens and Jim was determined they would build his Chelsea garden. So the logistics were becoming increasingly challenging and the costs were continuing to rise. They soon realised they would have to source the plants in England. Chelsea is first and foremost a 'horticultural' show. Garden design and quality construction is vital, but the quality of the plants is critical. They must be perfect to even begin to register with the judges—as well as the green-fingered and garden-wise British public. Quarantine regulations forbade the shipment of plants by air so the plants would have to be grown in England. The plant selection and the long program of nurturing and careful cultivation—so necessary to bring the plants to their peak during that week of the Chelsea show—would have to begin soon.

The realisation that someone would have to fly to England to reconnoitre the entire situation dawned on them early in the first week following that luncheon decision. And, they reasoned, whoever went would have to be there in time for the Chelsea show—only three weeks away! But who should make the journey? Clearly Jim's attendance, as designer, was critical. Wes is the nurseryman on the team, and since he has international experience importing and exporting rootstock, and has both personal and business relationships with leading British nurseries, his inclusion was obvious. As construction manager, Martin had to check possible sites and observe the whole build-up process. This only left Mark to stay behind and mind the shop, but Martin didn't agree. He argued that if he had broken his leg, for instance, some time between then and the following May, Mark would have taken charge of construction. So Mark, too, had to walk over the ground at Chelsea.

Martin and Anne had made the initial phone call to the RHS. Jim remembers, 'They got on the phone one night after the Melbourne show and spoke to Clare Green, who was the assistant shows manager in London. She was very excited that Australians were planning on coming. It was probably her enthusiasm that clinched our decision to go.' Since Mark would be the team member continuing the long and complicated negotiations with RHS—necessary to get them accepted—Martin believed he should be there to establish some sort of relationship. Four people meant four return airfares to London: the project's first real expenditure. Some early attempts had been made to secure an airline as a sponsor, but to no avail. It was decided that Martin would leave a week earlier than the others, so he could observe the full extent of the Chelsea build-up.

Before Martin could leave Melbourne they had to be sure they could actually gain entrance to the build-up and to the show itself. As Jim explained, 'Mark rang the RHS to tell them we were very keen on the possibility of maybe displaying at Chelsea, that we were flying over to have a look, and to see if it was possible to get passes for the show and build-up; at that late stage you can't buy tickets.' The RHS's initial enthusiasm for an Australian garden at the 2004 show seemed to have waned a little. Jim remembers, 'In a rather English manner they were polite but distant, reserved, and not very helpful. I guess you can't blame them—getting this strange call from Australia, cadging tickets, talking about displaying at Chelsea. They'd be thinking, "Well, good on you. You and the rest of them."' Perhaps Clare Green's initial enthusiasm for an Australian exhibit had been something of a PR exercise, somewhat 'front-of-house'. But, ultimately, the tickets and passes came through.

Martin was the first to arrive in London, and the first of the team to visit the show's long-established venue, in the grounds of the Royal Pensioners' Hospital. 'Chelsea has an incredible aura. It's an incredible event. It's the America's Cup of the gardening world. It captures the whole of England, and it captures the gardening world. In Melbourne, people would say, "That's a nice garden, but would it win a gold medal at Chelsea? Have you been to Chelsea?"' But Martin was not overwhelmed by what he was seeing. 'Everyone paints it as the big Holy Grail of garden shows, so that was a bit daunting. When you see them on the BBC and see them on the TV specials they look amazing. I'm sure they are, but to me, having seen them built I know they're sets, just like we can build. I know all the tricks. So having seen them built, I'm not afraid of Chelsea.' Martin spent those four or five days watching everything and talking to everyone. An English collegue, Bryan Sparling, recorded hours of activity on the video camera, and as he filmed he added a quiet, rather cynical commentary of his own: not everything he was observing was impressing him all that much. Perhaps his comments give some clue to their state of mind; perhaps they reflect something of Martin's mood at the time. Martin felt confident they could build to the best Chelsea standard. He felt confident that Jim's design, with its firewood wall and other unique features, would catch the interest of the British public. But the sheer scope of the show, with its 600 exhibits and its formidable reputation may have been beginning to depress him.

Mark, Jim and Wes arrived for the last weekend of the Chelsea build-up; Martin and Bryan picked them up at Heathrow. Jim remembers, 'Mark and Wes and I were quite excited at the time. But Marty was standing there and I could tell by his expression that things weren't good, and I think Mark felt the same thing. It was quite deflating. We expected Marty to be quite pumped up about the whole thing; he was the opposite. I think he realised that the project was even bigger than he'd dreamed of, and was beginning to believe that everything was against us. So, from the moment we arrived, mentally we were quite deflated.' Jetlag would not have been helping. 'We stopped building ourselves up for the show and went there feeling quite intimidated.' They had secured an interview with Mavis Sweetingham, the RHS event manager at Chelsea. 'We went to see her in the management office on the site. We were all in suits. She shook our hands and said, "Good to see you. I hope you enjoy the show." And that was about it. On the one hand we were a little disappointed at her reaction, but on the other hand it was quite good for us, because it kept it very real. We didn't get carried away with any excitement or false expectations. We also realised we were, perhaps, one of dozens of prospective exhibitors inquiring about Chelsea.'

The team was there to do a job, and despite their misgivings they settled into it. 'During build-up, you don't have the public in there. It's very hectic, very busy, but it's only the designers, the contractors, the nursery people and the event organisers there. Lots of lorries, heaps of deliveries. But it's quite easy to walk around and soak it in and get an idea of what's going on. Instantly, Bency and Marty were switched on together in construction mode. Their brains were ticking over, watching how things were being built. Bency's watching deliveries, how long it takes to get trucks in. They were introducing themselves to people and talking to them, listening to their comments about the battles they're going through. I was just taking in the extent of the designs: the styling and the finish and the detail and marvelling at how far they were taking these gardens.' Although Jim was planning that his garden had to be 'Australian-inspired', if only to justify its existence, he was already realising that to appeal to the British public on a deeper level than mere novelty, he had to quickly absorb something of the flavour of an English garden in England. 'You realise what the English obviously like to see in their gardens: they're very plants-based, and all their gardens look like they've been there for a long time.

'That first day we stopped for morning tea in a little food set-up for the tradesmen during the build-up. We had coffee and a biscuit,' and Jim began sketching in his journal how he would change the Melbourne garden. 'I always knew it had to be bigger and better; it had to be improved.' The site would be larger, for one thing. 'I knew I had to add more to it. I couldn't quite work out how I would use the rammed earth walls again. It couldn't be a courtyard, because we were doing a Chelsea show garden; it was too big to be a courtyard.' Jim knew they could excavate at Chelsea; they couldn't excavate in Melbourne. 'Maybe we could sink the courtyard part of the garden down two or three steps; turn it into a sunken garden.' They also discovered they had to include a service cum storage area at the back with a gate. 'I was struggling to work out how I was going to use the rammed earth walls. So I started scribbling. I think I came up with the idea of having an arbour walk beside the Melbourne design, and playing with the shape of river pebbles set into the paving.' The style of planting Jim observed in the English gardens was already influencing his embryonic design: 'In my head I knew the sort of planting I wanted to do. It had to have more of a "garden" feel; there had to be more plants, influenced by the English style of planting. But I knew these plants would have to reflect an Australian feeling, at least.'

Chelsea isn't called a 'flower show' for nothing. Coming out of their winter season, the British public is looking forward to seeing wonderful floral material when they come to Chelsea, flowers in the show gardens and masses of flowering material in the hundreds of floral displays. There were almost no flowers in Jim's gold-medal Melbourne garden; green foliage was the prominent plant material, there to soften the impact of the dramatic construction. 'Coming out of my Tuscan era of design, I was playing around with planting schemes that had a bit more of an Australian feel.' Jim had been experimenting. 'At our house down in Flinders I put in some silver foliage plants to see how they went. I don't really look after them down there. I like to push plants to see how they perform without much care—a plant will probably always look good if it looks good in that situation. So I was playing around with a lot of burgundy-coloured foliage and silver foliage and native grasses. But it's not a native garden.' Jim was looking more for a colour scheme that suggested the feel of an Australian landscape, rather than a garden of indigenous shrubs and trees. 'So the planting was going to be very different from what I did in Melbourne. The Melbourne planting was very green, using evergreen foliage. For Chelsea I wanted to do something that was more Australian in feel, using this silver and burgundy foliage and with blacks and browns in the grasses, mixed with plants that happen to be green. Plants that I knew would go well with rammed earth walls and the pebbles and pavers and the rusted steel pots. I wanted the whole styling of it to work well together; I was already convinced of that.' So it was still about foliage rather than flowers.

'I knew the firewood wall had such a strong impact. It develops a three-dimensional perspective when it's stacked up. I thought of all the colours of that firewood. They vary so much—from blood-red claret colours to soft honey-yellow colours—and they change, according to whether it's wet or dry. Then there's the shade in the gaps between the logs. So I knew that strong colours would work in that setting. We hadn't seen any plants yet. We hadn't done any nursery visits. It was just that things were ticking over in my head about how I could approach this new design for Chelsea. At the end of the day we knew we had to crank up the design.' And they knew this would be possible. 'We couldn't excavate in Melbourne, but we knew we could excavate in Chelsea. We had a lot more scope with construction, so I knew I could let myself go a bit with the design, knowing that we could excavate and that the construction period is two weeks. And I knew I had more space. The Chelsea sites are about 12 metres by 12 metres.' Jim renewed his acquaintance with Julian Dowle. Julian was building a garden that reflected a corner of a landscape in the Yorkshire Dales, one of several show gardens based on a 'wild landscape' theme that had become quite fashionable —and controversial—in Britain. They could see that the standard of workmanship on his garden was outstanding. 'They were literally "sewing in" the plants,' Mark commented. Jim introduced Julian— multiple Chelsea gold-medal winner—to Martin, Mark and Wes. He was to have quite an important, positive impact on the *Australian Inspiration* team before their visit was over.

No matter what fears were plaguing the others, Jim was feeling a little more confident by the end of that first day. Apart from beginning to bring his new design together in his head, he was observing a certain tardiness in the way the English crews worked, compared with what he knew happened in Australia. This was the Sunday, and judging would take place on the Monday. 'Remembering this was in the last three days of build-up, some of them seemed quite relaxed and I think that Australians would be putting a little bit more into it; they'd be a little more energetic. Sometimes if it began raining (and it rained quite a lot, right through the 2003 show) you'd notice them knocking off and having a cup of tea. Australians don't do that. If it

rains you keep on working.' The team were determined to bring
their own wheelbarrows. 'It seemed quite funny to see their old-
fashioned wheelbarrows, some with iron-rimmed wheels. We
thought that they'd love our rubber-tyred wheelbarrows.' And by the
end of the day they were even more determined to bring their own
construction team. Not that they had ever seriously considered any
alternative. They always knew their crew would come from the
Semken Landscaping workforce, noted for their experience with
show gardens, their skills, their high energy level, their enthusiasm,
their indomitable team spirit and their all-round determination to
win gold. They would need a team of at least 12 people: 12 return
Melbourne to London airfares!

At the end of that first day they went to a pub, had a few quiet
drinks and thought about it all. Jim remembers their subdued mood:
'We thought this is serious, this is very hard. Our chances now had
gone from what we thought were reasonably high to quite low. We
accepted the fact that the chances of us actually being accepted by
the RHS were very low. Not zero, but we'd be very lucky to get in.
We were a bit deflated by it all. I think we were all privately asking
ourselves if we were up to it. It's just such a big deal and we didn't
count on it being such a big deal. We started wondering whether the
show garden category was a little beyond us. Coming all that way
from Australia, should we do the Melbourne garden as a small
garden at Chelsea?' (The Chelsea Flower Show has categories for
smaller gardens.) 'We started to really think through and discuss all
these things and all the problems finally came back to funding. Who
was going to pay for it all? It's all very well to say that you want to do
Chelsea, but you need a lot of money.' Twelve airfares is just the
beginning, plus accommodation in London, probably one of the
most expensive cities in the world. 'The people who warned us

about the dollars we'd need were right on the money. There wouldn't be much change out of $300,000. That's a lot of money for a garden that's only going to be open to the public for four days. It's stupid, in many ways. We realised we were all carrying a fair load of stress. Who were we kidding? How the hell were we going to get this thing funded? To their credit, Fleming's had agreed to support us right up front. The idea was that Fleming's would underwrite the project with the full knowledge that sponsorship would be "on-sold" to others; whoever that may be. So far our efforts had been largely unsuccessful.'

On the Tuesday, the team left London in a hired car and drove to Northampton to visit Bill Swaney, who built rammed earth walls. It had been decided quite early that if rammed earth walls were to be included in the Chelsea garden, they would have to be built in England: the cost of shipping and likelihood of damage, quite apart from a probable quarantine problem, mitigated against bringing them from Melbourne. Bill was originally from Australia and was the brother of the business partner of Rick Lindsay, who built the Melbourne walls, and so the team felt a close affinity with Bill, especially Jim: 'He's an absolute gentleman and lives in a beautiful old manor house. Bill put on a beef and Guiness pie and a chicken pie for us for lunch. A fantastic lunch, as it was quite a cold day.' After lunch they walked around the garden, with Jim's digital camera recording every plant they saw. They also inspected several buildings with rammed earth walls Bill had built in the grounds, including a large barn where a number of rammed earth samples were laid out. The team was impressed by their quality; Jim was excited: 'He had about five or six different types of rammed earth, which had different colours in them. He added grey cement or off-white cement to get different colour combinations. I picked an ironstone with an off-white cement; it probably had a little more yellow in it than the one we had in Melbourne. It had a gritty, earthy look to it, a very natural, gutsy look. I knew that was definitely the one.' Meeting Bill and seeing his walls lifted their spirits somewhat. 'I think we felt that if we put in an order for rammed earth walls for Chelsea, he'd come through with the goods. He's not the sort of person who'd let us down. We knew we could ship almost everything from Australia, and we were confident about that. And we knew that we could get rammed earth walls. But all the plants had to be sourced over there, and that was a worry.'

The following day, the Wednesday, they set off on the first of their nursery visits, heading for Ipswich in Suffolk to view Notcutts Nursery. 'I'm looking at fields of plants and I'm straight away thinking about these colour schemes: burgundy and silver. I had my pad, pen and digital camera. What's that plant? Right, got it. Write down the name. A lot of them I knew, but a lot of variety names are a little different. It's like you're collecting 150 different genus of plants and out of that you might be using 50 of them. I was just short-listing, to take back to Melbourne as a database for the design process. I'm looking at plants for their foliage colour.' That evening they drove due east to spend the night at Lavenham, also in Suffolk, Bryan's home village. Originally a medieval wool town, it has declined in population and importance, but is now well-known as one of England's finest medieval 'black and white' timber-framed villages. Jim was greatly taken by the style and feeling of the village, suspecting that several of its most charming corners and features could be picked up in future show garden designs.

They left Lavenham at 6.30 the following morning as they had quite a way to go, travelling south-east to Hampshire, to the Hillier nursery at Ampfield, outside Southampton. The Fleming family has a close personal relationship with Robert Hillier, going back many years. Jim tells us, 'Hillier Nurseries are very traditional growers and their speciality is trees, but they grow shrubs as well. They've got an arboretum—a forest of trees from all over the world; not many nurseries have an arboretum. We met Robert Hillier, Wes had met him before, and we liked him. He was well-respected—very much your old English family breeding—he didn't seem like the person who'd stuff us around. Hillier Nurseries have a good reputation. We had seen their plants at the Chelsea show and we knew their quality was good, so we were keen on Hillier before we'd even met them. They were accommodating without being committed.' After all, the Australians still hadn't been accepted at Chelsea. 'We also met Ricky Dorlay, who's done 38 Chelsea shows. Hillier have a big nursery display in the marquee every year, and Ricky's in charge of all of Hillier's plants at the show. We felt very comfortable that Ricky knew what Chelsea is about, and if he was going to be in charge of growing, then we had 100 per cent faith in him.' The garden was coming together.

Hillier even had gum trees, including two varieties of snow gums. 'They were very attractive gum trees about four metres tall. They're quite mature and multi-stemmed; they're amazingly healthy. I thought well, bugger me, I never thought you'd see mature eucalypts for sale at a growing nursery in England. I thought, there's something in this; it feels good. We can get eucalypts, we can get rammed earth walls, and I'm seeing all these other colour schemes of plants that are going to work well too.

'By the time we had been through their nursery we were quite keen. Fleming's wanted to continue developing a relationship with Hilliers, Wes was very keen on working with Hillier, and certainly the three of us were happy to be going with Hillier. We knew they'd be our first pick.'

They were driving back to London when the question of what to call their Chelsea garden was first mooted. They considered what the garden meant and what words best described its spirit. Jim 'threw in "Inspirations of Australia", or something like that. Everyone thought there was something in that. It was a good way to describe what we were doing. We weren't doing an Australian native garden, but we were doing something that evoked feelings about Australia.' Something that was inspired by Australia. They threw this backwards and forwards, polished off the rough edges and the title *Australian Inspiration* was born.

The Australian team was back at the Chelsea show for the last day of the show. They 'conned' their way into one of the corporate hospitality tents and spent the afternoon drinking Pimms and listening to a brass band. On the last evening they have a 'sell-off'. They ring this big brass bell at 4.30pm and the public can buy things from all the gardens and displays. Julian Dowle had been especially kind and encouraging to the Australians through the week, offering advice and moral support. Jim remembers, 'We had dinner with him during the week, and Julian said he hadn't done a sell-off for a few years, and would we be interested in helping him. We thought that would be a great experience. We were all in suits that day and we turned up at Julian's garden at about four o'clock. Julian was quite shocked that we were in suits, but we said we didn't care. Julian had a little post office building as part of his garden, so we went inside and had a drink and a sandwich. Then we hung up our jackets, rolled up our sleeves and got out there. Marty was wearing a moneybag and Marty and I were out the front, bartering and selling plants to the public. Bency was in the garden with a shovel in his hand, digging down and lifting out these wisteria pots with mud all over him, while Marty and I were yelling out, having jokes with the English people. There were big corporate marquees overlooking the garden and women were drinking champagne and yelling out to us: "How much for that plant, and do you Aussie blokes come with it?" It seemed like there were 500 people crowded around watching us, with the BBC filming, and Bency's in there with the shovel, and Marty's rattling his bag of money, and the crowd's yelling out, and Julian's selling plants, when suddenly there's this crack of thunder. We looked up and this Concorde just dropped out of the clouds, almost hanging there, on its approach to Heathrow. All the English are used to this, but we're just standing there fascinated, looking up at this Concorde. I'd never seen a Concorde before. It would have made a great photo.' Suddenly London seemed a better place and the Chelsea Flower Show seemed more inviting.

Jim and Wes had been to London before, but for Martin and Mark it was a new experience. They managed to squeeze in some sightseeing, despite the tight schedule of their busy week. For Jim, 'The reconnaissance was a great experience. But doing Chelsea is not just about Chelsea. You're in London, the Mother Country. There's all these myths and legends you've heard so much about. You drive past Buckingham Palace and you think that the Queen lives there. There's the double-decker buses and Trafalgar Square and it's hard not to get swept away by the romance of it all. We realised that when we fly the guys over—if we get in—that they'd need a day just to focus on all this stuff. Then they could focus back onto the garden, because it's hard not to get overawed by it all.'

Jim didn't get much sleep on that interminably long plane journey back to Australia. 'On the flight back I sat up drawing this concept in my journal.' He had the arbour in place along one side, with its decorated pebbled walkway. He had the sunken garden and, of course, the rammed earth walls and the friendly domesticity of the firewood stack wall. In his head was the silver, burgundy and green foliage, set off against the lean, pale, multi-stemmed trunks of the Snow Gums (*Eucalyptus pauciflora* subsp. *niphophila*): all so Australian to us; all so exotic to the British public. 'I'd wake Bency and Marty up now and then and say, "What do you reckon about this?" While they were interested, they were exhausted. We'd lived on four or five hours sleep a night. "Yeah, that's great, Jim; whatever; whatever. I'm going back to sleep now. Yeah, that's good." But I do remember Marty looking at me and he gave me the wink: "You're on the right track there, that looks good."

chapter eight

An away game

ON THEIR RETURN from London, Jim Fogarty knew that the
coming weeks and months were vital. It was his responsibility to
design a garden that would gain them entry into the Chelsea Flower
Show. Martin Semken had said he knew that Semken Landscaping
had the skills and determination to build a Chelsea medal-winner:
'It's up to you to design a medal-winning garden now.' Jim knew he
was part of the way to achieving that goal. He had overwhelming
confidence in his Melbourne garden. It wasn't a fluke. It had taken
all three major awards at MIFGS. It had earned its accolades and the
right to go to Chelsea. Jim began re-designing that garden on the
morning he arrived at Chelsea. Allowing for the increased size of the
site, he began sketching ideas during their first morning coffee
break. The embryo of the arbour walk is there, though somewhat
truncated. The ability to excavate, denied them in Melbourne,

meant that he could begin thinking on several levels. The possibility of a sunken garden was already nudging out the Melbourne court-yard garden concept. The sketch plan that was created on their flight home, scribbled by Jim as he sat hunched up in an airline seat, working with a ballpoint pen by the light of the aircraft reading light, is remarkably close to the final design. The positions of the various elements would be arranged and re-arranged again and again, the details would be defined and refined many times over, but the basic concept is there, the inspirations that created it sure and certain. It is a work of artistic confidence. For Jim, first ideas are often the best.

As soon as he arrived back in Melbourne, Jim downloaded all the digital images he had taken of the plants into his computer. He busily identified and named them, creating a database that would be an invaluable reference for the months ahead. He also downloaded all the images he had taken of the many show gardens, right through their construction stages and from various angles when they were finished. 'I wanted to keep looking at them, realising how high I had to aim and how hard I had to push myself.' He used the concept plan he'd drawn on the plane, got it down to scale and that became the base plan. Jim then sat down and started developing the internal lay-out, working with the three areas he'd schemed on the flight back. The entire Melbourne garden became the largest of these areas and the idea of split-levelling the garden evolved in London. 'On the way back on the plane I realised it wasn't a courtyard garden any more,' restrained within tight boundaries, complete in itself. So the Melbourne garden—essentially an outdoor room—became the sunken garden and part of a larger, though still contained, land-scaped garden. Jim saw how he could justify retaining the rammed earth walls: they were now a design and engineering imperative, acting as retaining walls above the sunken garden. 'I knew a sunken garden would have a lot more interest. You can have steps down into it; then steps back up. You've got two levels of the garden to play with, and the firewood would frame it well.'

The second area of the re-designed garden was the arbour walk, made possible by the larger site. Paved with the specially made bluestone-coloured and granite pavers, the arbour walk is a long, pergola-like structure running the full depth of the site, with a step up off 'street' level. The path features the swash-like design of chocolate-brown Mansfield river pebbles of varying sizes, set into a charcoal-coloured, black oxide concrete slurry. 'The garden was quite square and geometric, and it had these curved jarrah benches designed and built by the furniture maker, Matt Heritage, in Bendigo.' The shape of these benches inspired the shape of the pebbled path, so the floor of the arbour looks 'like a gentle bend in a dry river bed'. The arbour walk leads to the third area of the garden, which Jim calls his 'secret garden'. Mostly hidden from view behind a section of the firewood wall, a path of rectangular 'steppers', cast to match the pavers, runs across the back of the site, ending in another water feature. Beyond this, but hidden from the secret garden by the firewood wall, is a small toolshed. The toolshed is an RHS requirement, accessed from outside the site. 'I didn't want to separate that third space, the secret garden, from the main garden, so I put a "window" in the firewood wall, behind the lounge area, so you can see it from the front of the site, right across the sunken garden. That works really well, tying in the two water features, and the window behind the lounge area is going to give the garden a lot of depth and perspective.'

On their return to Australia the team had about four weeks to complete their first submission and get it to London by post. So as soon as they got back they began having Chelsea team meetings almost on a weekly basis. They decided on their separate roles: Jim as designer, Martin as construction manager, Mark as logistics manager, evolving into team manager, and Wes as project coordinator, looking after the non-gardening peripherals. 'There were so many things to cover,' Jim says. Perhaps the most urgent element demanding attention was finance. 'We'd seen Chelsea now, so we knew we were talking about pretty big dollars needed to get it all off the ground. Without financial backing there was no way we were going to do it.' So chasing sponsorship became their first priority. 'Initially, we were all banding together with various ideas and contacts. We very quickly put a proposal together.' This was a full-colour printed booklet with numerous photographs of the Melbourne garden, brief statements of intent, potted biographies of the principals and their impressive show garden credentials, and a detailed projected budget. Mark Bence had costed the whole thing: the materials involved and the cost of going over there to do it, and with everything included, including airfares, shipping costs and accommodation in London, the bottom line ran to more than $280,000. Fleming's briefed their PR consultants to produce this document and chase up initial sponsorship leads. They even created an *Australian Inspiration* logo. 'From the beginning Fleming's—and Wes in particular—supported the whole project. To Wes's credit they became the underwriters. They were going to back it if no one else did. Wes and his family put their money where their mouth is. Without Fleming's backing we wouldn't have got as far as we've got.'

The first move was to try and interest major sponsors from outside the horticultural industry. It was a hard road. Jim reckons, 'The idea of show gardens in Australia just isn't news.' Gardening isn't 'sexy'. They tried airlines, at least to help them with fares, and explored the possibility of promoting the garden as an Australian beer garden, to perhaps interest a big brewing company. 'Chelsea's a champagne and wine show, so there's all the wine companies and wine exporting companies.' All their efforts outside the horticultural industry were proving fruitless. They tried everybody. 'I spoke on the phone to a young marketing girl from a well-known paint company. I've used their products a lot. She'd never heard of Chelsea and basically had no interest in even giving us paint—not even 500 bucks worth of paint. You can't blame them. They get a lot of people wanting free things.' The team soon realised that a big motivation for taking the garden to Chelsea was to garner a high level of media, public and corporate interest by succeeding overseas. The sponsorship apathy they were confronting was a real indication of their industry's low level of public awareness. They needed Chelsea to get the money; but they needed the money to get to Chelsea. 'It told us we were breaking new ground. You can't get pissed off or disappointed because someone's not giving you money or product. We're the first people doing this Chelsea thing. It's the same with media here. It's all an unknown. Maybe after we've done it, people might come up to us and say, "Hey, why didn't you come and ask me for paint? We would've given you paint—and cash." The reality is, until you've done it, it is new territory and we are going out on a limb.'

They were on much surer ground when they approached people in the horticultural industry. 'When you add up the cost of materials that could be obtained from product sponsors, you're talking about quite a lot of money. So naturally the first thing we had to do was to consider all the players involved in the Melbourne garden, and give them first right of refusal to be part of this process, which we did. Now all the hard materials for *Australian Inspiration* are supported by all the same people who supported us in Melbourne: pavers, pots, furniture, general landscape supplies, tools, even wheelbarrows! So the team has stayed together.' But they still lacked major corporate sponsors. 'People said you're not going to get sponsorship for this, and Wes's attitude was, "If no one else will pay for it, we bloody-well will, and we'll make sure this happens." Full credit to them. Fleming's have been great from day one.' At some point along the way the team accepted reality and Fleming's agreed to make their role official, and accepted the position of 'naming sponsor'. The garden became known as *Fleming's Nurseries Australian Inspiration*. As well as Fleming's making a major commitment, Jim Fogarty Design Pty Ltd and Semken Landscaping were donating major portions of their services to the project. The Melbourne International Flower and Garden Show had also committed a quite substantial sum of money. 'It was good to have their support. We were very keen, right from the beginning, to represent the Melbourne International Flower and Garden Show. It wasn't just about us. We wanted to do it as a team thing. So we were very pleased to represent the Melbourne show as well.'

Despite the long hours spent preparing plans and a written submission for their Chelsea bid, the *Australian Inspiration* team found time to make major contributions to a remarkable, heart-warming project. Very Special Kids is a charity that provides palliative care for children dying of cancer, and they run a hospice in the Melbourne suburb of Malvern. One of their major sponsors is the insurance company, IOOF, which is also the principal sponsor of the Melbourne International Flower and Garden Show; IOOF's CEO, Rob Turner, is also a friend of Martin Semken. The land in front of the hospice consisted mainly of grass, concrete paths and a conventional children's playground. IOOF was looking to finance a 'sensory' garden to be built on this rather uninspiring area; Richmond Football Club was also involved, as IOOF is one of their sponsors as well. Jim was commissioned by IOOF to design the sensory garden, and he re-designed the rest of the garden as a donation. Semken Landscaping agreed to build it—with manual labour supplied by the footy club—and to complete the Chelsea team connection, Fleming's—already a major Very Special Kids sponsor—agreed to supply all the plants. For the team, Chelsea was still just a fantasy— they hadn't even been accepted. 'You could have all these pipe dreams, but every time we went down to Very Special Kids we'd realise the realities of life and we'd appreciate how lucky we are. For Fleming's Nurseries, Semken Landscaping and Jim Fogarty Design it was nice to put back. Very Special Kids is dealing with the reality of life and death. And with Chelsea we were asking so many people for help, so it was nice to put something back.'

The idea of the sensory garden, as Jim saw it, was to provide pleasure and stimulation for these children through their last months and weeks; right up until that time when they were unable to leave their beds. IOOF have a tall office building, right in the heart of Melbourne's business district; on the roof is a large neon sign that lights up in green all night. This became Jim's inspiration for the core of the design. 'I remember when I was young it was really popular to have those glow-in-the-dark stars and moons that you'd stick on the ceiling of your bedroom.' So Jim designed 'a little city centre with six little skyscrapers, the tallest was one and a half metres high and we had them all lit up. Glenn McGrath from Light on Landscape—he's doing Chelsea with us—he provided all the labour and equipment for lighting. At night, they go from pink to yellow, then green. I think for these kids, night-time is probably the loneliest time—in a hospice, lying in bed, looking out the window. It provides a little theatre for them. As well as that we had water features they could touch, and we had strawberries and apples and mint and plants they could eat, touch and smell, and pathways built of cobbles and pebbles.

'As well as the sensory garden there's a special playground they shipped in from overseas. They've got sandpits, some built so that a wheelchair can go right in and the kids can sit there and play, like at a kitchen table. We put in a lot of plants and shade trees, and we built a Humpty Dumpty on a wall. There are topiary pigs, honouring the Piggy Bank Appeal for Very Special Kids. And it's not just for the kids—it's also for their families. There's a new barbecue built in, with a mosaic with the Very Special Kids logo in the paving. Lots of the kids are in wheelchairs, so there's wheelchair access the whole way through. And for those who can't even get into a wheelchair, we provided visuals for them to look at through the windows. A lot of other companies involved in Chelsea donated product as well: Cast In Stone donated pavers that glowed in the dark, and Daisy's Garden Supplies donated a lot of material. We had all the Semken Landscaping people, plus bricklayers and plumbers who donated their time. At the end of the day there was a garden worth about $150,000, all costing nothing. You're talking about guys who don't make a lot of money, guys who make a living at hard physical work; and there they were on their weekends and days off, doing what they did down there. Very Special Kids was the reality of the power of people banding together and working as a team.'

Meanwhile, the due date for the receipt of their initial Chelsea submission—detailed plans and documentation—was drawing inexorably closer. Jim explains that the team had to answer numerous questions 'about the theme of the garden and even why we wanted to display at Chelsea—questions you never think you'd be asked, but I think they're trying to suss out how serious you are. They also asked questions about the financials and who's paying for it.' And this submission was merely a preliminary skirmish to see if *Australian Inspiration* would be permitted to actually apply for a show garden site. 'It's pretty competitive. Perhaps out of 80 applications they might pick 50,' who would proceed to the next stage, to compete for one of the 21 show garden sites available in 2004. 'We learned around this time that New Zealand also had a submission in. At first we were a little disappointed. We wanted to be the first show garden from the region. But now we're really happy that New Zealand is having a show garden there as well.

'On August 18 we were accepted into the first round. They then called for further specific information, including more design details. They wanted cross-sectional elevations, which means you put an imaginary breadknife through the whole garden and then draw it out with all its dimensions. They're very strict about the boundary treatments at Chelsea. There's rules and regulations about how high your walls are at the front, and how they step up, because they obviously affect the next show garden. The overall aesthetics of the avenues are policed, making sure there are no big walls coming right out to the pathways. When we were told we had been accepted into the first round, we were only given about two weeks for the final plans and documentation to be submitted. They were sent on August 30. We were then told we would find out if we were going to Chelsea some time in September, which is when the sites would be allocated.'

In September, before word from London came through, Jim was commissioned to design a show garden in Sydney. It was the first year of 'Sydney in Bloom'. There had been garden shows in Sydney before, but this was the first time actual show gardens were featured. 'I was employed as designer and I got Semken Landscaping involved. CSR were the sponsors; they paid. But it was a limited budget, so we still got some product donated. It was a really good experience, because Marty, Brad Peeters, David Nichol and I went up to Sydney, and we were there for just over two weeks. We drove up in two utes and we took up all the tools. This was our first test at an "away game". We didn't go up there to compete with anyone; we went up to compete with ourselves. The pressure was on us and we knew, if we didn't do well in Sydney, maybe this whole Chelsea thing was just a pipedream. But if we went well in Sydney, it was going to give the Chelsea project legs. Marty was on a mission—he was very focused, and so was I. Even though this was a smaller event, smaller garden, no fanfare at all, we knew we were going up there to test ourselves. You couldn't drive back to the yard to pick up something you'd forgotten, and out of all the tools the boys packed into the two utes, the only thing they forgot was a hacksaw. A lot of other people were even borrowing Semken Landscaping's tools!'

Sydney in Bloom for 2003 was staged in the middle of the city, in the Domain in beautiful weather. Jim reckons, 'It was a great setting. You've got Centrepoint Tower and the whole of Macquarie Street right there above you. It was part of the Royal Botanic Gardens, so you couldn't excavate; you weren't even allowed to drive pegs into the ground. The garden was totally different to the Melbourne award-winner and the one I was designing for Chelsea. It was a very modern garden, very bold, very architectural, with very strong colours: bluestone, dark-chocolate brown and a sort of biscuit

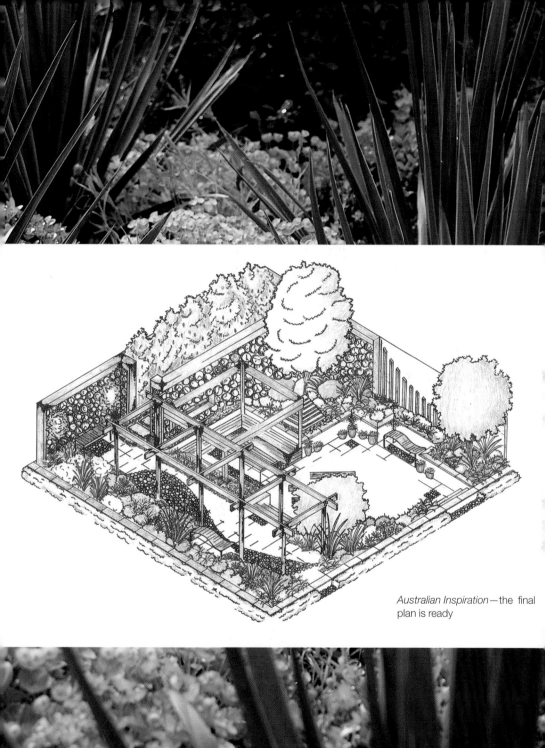

Australian Inspiration — the final
plan is ready

ABOVE Melbourne's Lord Mayor Cr John So and the sponsors farewell the team. BACK ROW FROM LEFT TO RIGHT Paul Stammers, Brad Peeters, Mark Stammers, Jim Fogarty, Cr So, Mark Bence, Wes Fleming, Anne Semken, Glenn McGrath, Andrew Triantafillou, David Brown, Mandy Bence, Adrian Clancy; FRONT Peter Barnard, Graeme Fleming, Matt Heritage.

RIGHT Jim and Mark with Ricky Dorlay at the main Hillier nursery.

OPPOSITE TOP Mark-out day at Chelsea. FROM LEFT Mark Stammers, Mark Bence, Martin Semken, Anne Semken, David Brown, Jim Fogarty, Bryan Sparling, Paul Stammers, Brad Peeters. 'Fat Guts' is on the digger.

OPPOSITE On your marks—Bryan, David, Brad, Paul and Jim.

LEFT Locating the corners—
Mark Stammers, Jim, Brad,
Paul, Marty's backside, Mark
Bence and David.

BELOW End of excavation.
Wheelbarrows have been
placed as a safety barrier
around the soakage pit.

ABOVE The first container arrives.

LEFT Unloading the rammed earth wall sections, each one made to measure.

Julian Dowle and Jim Fogarty.

ABOVE Filling the arbour walk with hardcore.

LEFT The rammed earth wall is put in place.

Out of the ground—the timber framework is ready for the firewood walls.

TOP LEFT Checking colour match for the grout.

TOP RIGHT Wes on the level—even the sponsor had to help.

ABOVE Unloading firewood from the blue container.

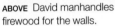

ABOVE David manhandles firewood for the walls.

ABOVE RIGHT 'Sitting' arbour posts on temporary footings.

RIGHT Jim and Glenn McGrath confirming final positions for light fittings.

OPPOSITE Stonemasons Brad Peeters and Mark Stammers building the firewood wall.

ABOVE Work in progress—Hebel blocks mark the front boundary, hardcore fills the arbour walk, the timber framing is completed and firewood walling underway.

LEFT Glenn McGrath contemplates lighting the water feature.

OPPOSITE The last two logs are placed; the window is in position.

ABOVE RIGHT Every pebble is laid one at a time.

ABOVE Cursing the designer his pebble mosaic.

RIGHT Brad cuts the 'meander' pattern in the arbour walk pavers.

OPPOSITE Changing gear—Jim contemplates the planting phase.

ABOVE AND FAR LEFT Martin 'insulates' his team with the plant trolleys and then backs up the planting crew.

LEFT Mandy plants Australian wildflowers.

LEFT Paul plants the Box hedge along the front boundary.

BELOW Jim and Glenn place firewood wall lights; David plants the secret garden.

BOTTOM Planting alongside the arbour walk, Cabbage Trees in the foreground.

OPPOSITE Mark Stammers completes final window details.

LEFT Bryan and Mandy weave the honeysuckle through the steel mesh.

BELOW Glenn and Jim installing firewood wall lighting.

BELOW LEFT David paints the pots with diluted acid to enhance rusting.

RIGHT Positioning a Snow Gum with the tele-lifter.

BELOW Jim plant detailing; Tanya Clayton planting.

OPPOSITE Brad stains the Redgum lawn steppers.

NEXT SPREAD Barefoot styling— the final touches are made.

The 'outdoor room' looks inviting from every angle.

OPPOSITE Matt Heritage's 'Duckboard' bench nestles among the plants.

LEFT One of the black slate water features.

BELOW A Snow Gum rises through the Kangaroo Paws and Blue Fescue.

ABOVE Day of reckoning – RHS judges assess the garden.

LEFT The meander theme is picked up in a garden bench and the black posts on the right-hand boundary.

OPPOSITE Light and shade.

ABOVE Rhapsody in blue—the arbour walk at night.

RIGHT Looking good together—Lavender co-existing with White Anzac Bottlebrush.

Judge and jury—RHS show garden judging panel.

Medal morning—Anne Semken, David Brown, Mark Bence, Tanya Clayton, Martin Semken, Paul Stammers, Wes Fleming, Brad Peeters, Mandy Bence, Mark Stammers, Bryan Sparling, Glenn McGrath and Jim Fogarty with silver-gilt medal certificate.

Well done, Aussies! RHS president Sir Richard Carew Pole shares the moment with Martin Semken, Jim Fogarty, Mark Bence and Wes Fleming.

Celebrities all—British TV garden personality Alan Titchmarsh with Jim, Mark and Martin.

TOP *Australian Inspiration* meets HRH Queen Elizabeth.

ABOVE In celebration – *Australian Inspiration* realises its true potential.

colour. The plants were all from Warner's Nurseries, out of Melbourne and transported up by road. But they were all plants that would grow in Sydney, in sub-tropical conditions. The plants were very strong in foliage colours too: burgundy foliage and silver foliage. The only flowers were white.

'Fleming's lent us the tree, which they shipped up: a nice big feature tree, the only tree in the garden. It was a Honey Locust (*Gleditsia tricanthos* "Sunburst"). We were in early spring, so some of plants hadn't quite flowered. Of course Sydney is a lot warmer and we had the plants there from the beginning of build-up, so we had them set aside and were watering them every day. During the build-up the tree began to bud, then burst, and the flowers started opening because it was hotter up there and sunny every day. I was madly trying to time the plants: some that were cooking in the sun I had to put in the shade, and the ones that were shaded and which I wanted to flower—I'd bring out into the sun. We had azaleas that were just budding and budding and budding and I wanted them to burst for the first day of the show. Every day was crucial for the plants.

'It was an urban courtyard garden called *CSR–PGH City Living*.' Some older visitors to Sydney in Bloom commented that it reminded them of a 1950s–1960s garden. 'I hadn't thought of it like that, but I could see it. I had these white curving retaining walls coming out of this bluestone-coloured back wall. The retaining walls were chalk-white and they looked really crisp. The thing about show gardens is you're trying to draw a response from people. It may not be to every-one's liking—it's not necessarily my favourite garden. I liked the garden, but it was just a garden designed to bring forth comment, and the older generation liked it. It had a lot of plants like Lily of the Valley (*Pieris* sp.) and azaleas, more the style of planting from that period. Marty loved the garden, he was really proud of what he'd done with it, and he's got every right to be. The construction was beautiful. We even had a client come up from Melbourne.' He arrived at night. The surroundings were pitch black, but the garden had been lit—once more by Glenn McGrath from Melbourne. The client saw the 'quality finish. He loved it. He didn't even get another quote. He locked Semken Landscaping in to build his garden, before they'd even priced the job. That's unheard of.'

So there they were, in Sydney, building the CSR garden. It was the middle of September and 'at the back of our minds, we knew that any day we'd probably find out whether or not we were going to Chelsea. It was a difficult time for us in many ways. The PR people obviously knew that we had a submission in for Chelsea, and their job was to promote the Sydney show.' What better angle could they have than one of their exhibitors being selected for Chelsea? 'So every day they were asking, "Have you heard yet? Have you heard yet?" And we'd have to say, "No, no, we haven't heard a thing." We were constantly ringing Mark back in Melbourne. But he had heard nothing. The silence was deafening. Maybe they were just going to mail us a letter and we wouldn't know until October. Our first day on-site in Sydney was Sunday, September 14.' Early each morning Marty and Jim checked their emails, before heading off for the site. About 6am on Friday, September 19, Jim received an email from Julian Dowle. 'It read: "Jim, you may like to unofficially know that you've been accepted at Chelsea. Congratulations." It was great coming from Julian. He'd become a father figure, a mentor. It hits you right there. "Bloody hell, Marty, look at this!" But we knew it was unofficial, so we would have to be careful.' Jim and Martin rang Mark Bence immediately, and he replied, "I think until we get the letter, we'd better keep it quiet." However the PR people in Sydney were asking us every day, so we told them—unofficially. Next thing

you know, a *Sydney Morning Herald* journalist is down there inter-
viewing Marty and I, and for the first time we experienced exposure
outside the gardening media—this was a real journalist from a real
newspaper. It appeared on something like page four, about these two
blokes building a garden in Sydney, bound for Chelsea. It also made
The Age in Melbourne, with a small piece about the Australian gardeners off to Chelsea. It was a great weight off our shoulders.' They
realised this great project was now—actually—going to happen.

Despite these distractions, their first responsibility was to finish
this garden. 'We still had the last few days of set-up in Sydney to
complete, so Marty and I were still very focused. We knew it was
even more important that we achieved a good result on this garden,
so we really busted ourselves, and so did everyone working on it.' As
well as Marty and Jim and the two landscapers from Semken
Landscaping, they employed a paving contractor and several bricklayers. Once the hard construction was finished, the planting was
done by the key team. 'We weren't competing against anyone; but it
was a test of Marty's construction management. We were the first
show garden finished. We knew that at Chelsea we would have to
finish way before the completion time, because by Saturday and
Sunday there's media all over your garden, long before the official
media day. So Marty's aim in Sydney was to finish as early as possible
and we basically finished on the Monday night. On Tuesday morning we did the last bits and pieces: the furniture went in, pots, everything was watered, we cleaned up around the site and by lunch-time
we were having a cold beer, and we still had a few hours to go. Marty
got a lot of confidence out of that, remembering that the whole thing
was an away game. Bency was 990 kilometres away. The yard was
990 kilometres away. Everyone was 990 kilometres away.

'Next morning was the official breakfast. We were all in suits. I think some comments were made that we were a bit cocky, wearing suits. They read out the medal winners, starting from bronze. Marty and I were shitting ourselves, because everything was riding on this. If we didn't get a good result—for Bency back in Melbourne, and for Fleming's—they'd have been thinking, "You've stuffed this up, fellers. Are you the right people to be going to London? Maybe you're not." When they read out the gold, and we got the gold, it was such a huge relief. It wasn't about the competition, because everyone can get a gold medal if they get to that standard of finish. We had proven it to ourselves, and we nailed it. Everything went to plan. We had covered all the bases.'

chapter nine

A garden goes to sea

UNTIL THEY WERE accepted at Chelsea, the *Australian Inspiration* project barely existed in London. Jim knew, 'Until they've allocated the show garden, everybody is a nobody—unless you've already got a Chelsea history. We were nobodies from nowhere. We had won gold medals in Australia, but that didn't mean a lot to them. But getting accepted gave us a feeling we were being admitted into some sort of fraternity. Not that anything's said, but you do feel it. Their attitude to us warmed a lot more, and it all became a lot more real. You've got to pinch yourself now and then and think, "We are very fortunate. Now don't stuff this up. Don't take anything for granted."' The RHS had appointed a new Chelsea Flower Show event manager. 'Anita Collins had come in. She was a lot younger. In October we actually received the letter, on letterhead from the RHS, telling us that we had been accepted. Bency felt comfortable then; he wanted that letter. Until you get that letter on their official letterhead, you can't really act on anything. Having an unofficial email from Julian Dowle wasn't enough for Bency. He wanted the real thing.

'We got the site allocation with the letter, and that's when we discovered that the site was 10 metres deep, not 12.' The garden had to be re-designed again, and all the amended plans sent back to London. 'We had a matter of days to reconfigure the whole design and send it back so it arrived in early November. There was about 120 hours of drafting for each reconfiguration.' Jim was doing this for the third time. 'I had to cut two metres out of the garden.' And there was another problem to be faced: in its final allocated position, 'The garden now had to be viewed from the front and left, not front and right. I had to "mirror" the whole thing. That could be done, but it felt all left-handed. Only over time have I begun to feel comfortable with it.' This is when they also discovered they had to have a shed for the tools. 'It's not part of the garden, but you've got to have a service area. We've put the shed in our secret garden, and put the firewood wall around it, so you don't see it. The average punter will never notice that we've lost two metres, but I do. There was no way around it, so we just chopped out two metres and reconfigured the geometry of the garden to encompass that. The arbour walk is two metres shorter and the lawn area's now not so deep.'

Wes Fleming and Jim were flying out to London on Friday, November 10, and Jim was taking the new plans with him. 'So we were under the pump, big-time. We got the plans printed in the nick of time and then Wes and I flew out on our plant-sourcing trip.' Now they had been officially accepted they could make their final plant choices and confirm their nursery orders. They picked up a hire car and drove direct from Heathrow to Julian Dowle's house at Newent in Gloucestershire. Julian's wife Tessa had cooked roast beef and

Yorkshire pudding. 'One of my favourite meals,' Jim remembers fondly. Julian's son Peter was there. 'Pete's got a landscape construction business, and he's built a lot of Julian's Chelsea gardens, so he knows a lot about Chelsea.' Peter asked them to 'keep him in the loop' and he offered to give the Australians any help they might need at Chelsea. After dinner Jim sat up with Julian, drinking Drambuie and watching video presentations of some of Julian's show gardens. Julian told Jim, 'You people are now part of the Chelsea family.' Jim was beginning to feel accepted.

Next morning they left for Hillier's main nursery at Ampfield near Southampton in Hampshire. They needed to confirm Robert Hillier's support, as they needed Hillier's to grow most of their plants, under contract to Fleming's. They checked on the Snow Gums Jim had chosen in May, and they were doing well. But they knew they would have to look further afield for all the Australian species they would need. 'When they called for more detailed information after our first round acceptance, RHS said they would like to see more Australian plants in our garden. This was the first Australian garden, so they wanted more Australian plants. We knew that not every garden in Australia is an Australian native garden. Australia is a very diverse country, influenced by many regions of the world and therefore Australian gardens are very eclectic. There could be plants from anywhere in the world. We felt quite strongly that this garden should be an "Australian-inspired" garden, and while 50 per cent of our plants can be Australian, the others would be from different parts of the world. It might be a plant from England, but because of its silver or burgundy foliage, it suggested the colours or textures of Australia. Fleming's aren't a native nursery—they grow exotic trees—so we felt it was a fair reflection of an Australian garden to mix the plants. That was the case we put to them, and the RHS were happy with that.' But the problem of finding enough Australian plants in Britain was still with them.

'We knew we would have a battle trying to find Australian plants in England.' Quarantine would never allow them to import plants direct from Australia. 'None of us knew the industry in England well enough to know where we were going to get these plants.' They knew that Hillier had snow gums. 'We had seen them, and they had bottlebrushes, but as far as finding a broader range of Australian plants, the odds were against us.' They considered sourcing plants from the warmer climate of southern Europe, where quarantine regulations would not be a problem. 'We knew that in Portugal and Italy they grew some Australian plants. Wes had booked this flight into London, then out via Rome and anywhere in between. We didn't know what we were up against. We might have had to fly down to Portugal, then to Italy, source all these plants, then get them shipped back to Hillier for them to grow them.' It was an unnerving trip for Jim, 'Getting a plant list together for a show garden, you can go to one nursery, then everything can change. You think certain plants are okay, then later they might say, "We've sold out of those now." I had Redhot Pokers (*Kniphofia* sp.) in the design. It didn't take long to realise they're not going to be in flower for Chelsea.' But those Australian plants still eluded them. They only had 10 days and the problem was far from solved when they had to return home.

Before they left for Australia they met with Anita Collins in the RHS building in Vincent Square. Jim fondly remembers, 'That was a great moment. We went into this beautiful old building and Anita took us up into the boardroom.' Jim felt like he'd discovered the Holy Grail of gardening. 'This young Burnley student meeting with the Chelsea event director in the boardroom at the Royal Horticultural Society in London! A portrait of Sir Joseph Banks was over the fireplace. It was hard to pay attention to Anita.' She then raised the issue of the 'ring beam'. The original Great Marquee, which housed the indoor floral displays, was an immense, four-acre canvas structure, raised onto a forest of flag-topped poles. This was replaced in 2000 by two rigid Floral Pavilions; but in 2004 these would be combined to form the Great Pavilion. It is on the space vacated by one of these Floral Pavilions that the Australian garden would be sited. But long concrete footings, buried beneath the ground, anchored these pavilions—these are called the 'ring beams', and one of these runs through the site allocated to *Australian Inspiration*. Anita gave Jim details of the approximate position and depth of this foundation. 'I'm thinking, "What are we going to do now?" I've developed the sunken garden to sort out the rammed earth walls, and roughly 25cm beneath the ground is this footing we couldn't disturb. It was right underneath where the rammed earth walls were going to be. I didn't know how I was going to solve this problem.'

Jim was especially disappointed that this ring beam seemed to be making excavation difficult, as this was the big design advantage Chelsea had over Melbourne. 'I slept on it for days and worked out that perhaps we could build the garden above ground, then step down, so we'd clear this ring beam. I threw this at Bency when I got back and he agreed this was probably the only way around the prob-lem. We were playing with millimetres here. The way the steps and terracing worked, we needed 266mm from the existing ground down.' But they didn't know exactly where that ring beam was on their site, and they didn't know exactly how deep it was beneath the ground. The compromise Jim was suggesting might not be neces-sary; but they had to know. Meanwhile Jim was proceeding as though the beam was in the wrong place, just in case it was. 'So I had to redo the whole design, allowing for this ring beam and stepping the garden up a bit higher. I also had to redo the planting configuration, now that we'd sourced all these other plants, and send it all back to the RHS.'

On November 28 Jim travelled to New Zealand where he helped judge the Ellerslie Flower Show in Auckland, joining Julian Dowle on the panel. Mark Bence was also invited to judge, but he was far too busy to get away. Jim had begun scheduling all the materials for Chelsea. 'I do a preliminary list of all the materials involved in the design, which then goes to Bency. Mark pulls it all apart and quantifies all the materials. We then discuss any discrepancies and try to get it right. He's also organising quarantine issues and the shipping; all the logistics.'

The materials were all coming together. 'We'd confirmed the pavers—and Cast In Stone are on board. The furniture was coming from Matt Heritage in Bendigo, the lighting from Glenn McGrath of Light on Landscape, the recycled timber from Pete Barnard, and Paula Johnstone and Charlie Johnstone of Steel Living were doing the pots. The mulch came in from Bio Gro, Daisy's were donating other landscaping supplies and Reece were donating all the plumbing gear for the water features.' Although the rammed earth walls were still being built in England, at Bill Swaney's establishment in Northampton, they decided that Rick Lindsay from Mansfield would fly over and supervise their construction. 'Bill's got the set-up for them over there, but building them for our show garden is different. Fleming's are flying Rick over because he knows the game—he knows how we did it last time. And he's thinking of ways we might be able to retrieve the walls and have them re-used, instead of binning them. He's going to make another steel jib, which will be part of the reinforcing mesh inside the walls, so we can crane them and forklift them onto the site.

'We had our first construction meeting out at Molan Street in Ringwood in late November. We had Paul Stammers, Mark Stammers, Brad Peeters, Bency and myself; and David "Charlie" Brown who's going to be hands-on doing the planting. We pulled the plans apart—literally. We verbally built the garden and we discussed all the problems that might occur—what we might face, based on our experiences with the Melbourne garden.'

Meanwhile, the timber for the firewood walls was being collected. The team has been proud to say, over and over, 'Not a tree died for the building of those walls.' Adrian Clancy, of Statewide Tree Services, an arborist based in Warrandyte, had been collecting the timber over a number of months. As he did his work around Melbourne, each branch he had to lop, each dead or dangerous tree he had to take out, if the wood was suitable, it was carefully sawn into 30cm lengths and saved for Chelsea. When the author and his family shifted to Warrandyte 35 years ago and built a house on a bush block, we planted many small trees, including a tiny Lemon-scented Gum (*Corymbia citriodora*) we took from a tube and positioned along the front fence-line. It did well for a few seasons, but when it was a sapling about a metre and a half tall it appeared to die. But that was not the end of it. A few weeks later it sent out several shoots from its base, and soon these shoots—five of them in all—were growing well and the tree was taking on a 'mallee' shape with five trunks. The decades passed and this 'freak' tree with its five thick and healthy trunks grew and grew until its canopy covered half the front garden. It was a beautiful tree, admired by neighbours and visitors alike. Its pungent lemon scent was especially noticeable after rain or at the end of a hot, still day. But it was much larger—its trunks were now heavier than any mallee—and because the point where it sprouted—its heart—collected water and debris and began to rot, it became unstable. Its spreading canopy also threatened power lines. One of its heavy trunks fell, just missing a parked car. Another shattered in a high wind and fell across the road. It was unsafe, and early in 2004 Adrian Clancy declared it dangerous and obtained council permission to remove it. Adrian and his team worked carefully and methodically, taking out the canopy and then the trunks, piece by piece, not only because it could not be safely felled, but also so each length of this once beautiful tree could be cut into pieces and saved for Jim Fogarty's firewood walls.

Before the end of 2003, it was obvious that another trip to London was necessary. The London public relations firm Fleming's had hired was planning a media launch for five Chelsea gardens, including *Australian Inspiration*. As designer, Jim had to be present, as did Wes as sponsor. 'But it would have been nice to have one of the Semken Landscaping guys there. Wes wasn't keen on more than two of us going, for good reason: it was costing money. But Bency had issues he wanted to sort out.' Peter Dowle had offered his support with construction in London. 'It was best that Marty or Mark met with Peter Dowle. We also had to shift these containers from the docks at Tilbury, store them somewhere—maybe Hillier—and try and get all the gear up for Chelsea. If Bency could get the containers dropped off at the Chelsea site it was going to save us thousands of dollars in transport fees. So for the few thousand dollars to fly Bency over, it might actually save us 10 or 11 grand. It was decided Mark would fly with me and we'd have a meeting with Peter Dowle up in Newent, Gloucester.' Jim also knew that the international Ball company had a nursery in England that grew Australian plants. So they decided to go to Oxfordshire to sort out the Ball plants and then go down to Hillier.

Jim and Mark arrived at Heathrow and drove straight up to Gloucester. 'We had a two-hour meeting in Julian Dowle's office and Peter Dowle was fantastic. Bency had a page full of questions to ask and I just sat back.' Peter Dowle had an answer for every question and a solution for each problem. 'Bency felt so relieved after that. Peter had offered more than we could have expected: in support, in help and labour if we needed it. He'd be able to help us organising sands, soils and cements; all the stuff we're not shipping from Australia; hiring any machinery we needed; he offered the whole lot.' Then Mark asked the really hard question; the worst scenario they could think of: what happens if this container falls off the ship and we lose everything? Peter said, "Give me a list of all your materials and I'll keep them in mind. So you've lost all your pavers? I know where we can get more pavers, for instance." The three of us went through it all. It was the worst thing that could happen, but it was a remote possibility, and we were prepared for it.'

Jim decided that as well as the Australian plants that were being grown by Hillier, they still needed to locate the grasses and the wildflowers such as Outback Daisy (*Brachycome* sp.), Straw Flower (*Bracteantha* sp.) and the Outback Fan Flower (*Scaevola* sp.). 'These are more like rockery plants. They only grow about a foot high and a foot in diameter. You need these plants in a show garden as they cover up the gaps on the ground and next to your paving. It's that last touch that you need in a show garden. The planting needs to look full and established and mature, so if you've gaps and you can see any mulch, you're going to lose points. These plants are ground huggers and they're going to frame the paving and spill out onto the paving, adding that last two per cent that might get you over the ticker from silver to silver gilt, or from silver gilt to gold. Just that last little detail. We walked into this meeting with Stuart Lowen of Ball Colegrave in Oxfordshire to find a place to grow these plants. "We're battling here," we said. "We have a geographical problem. We can't bring these plants over ourselves. Can't you help us out?" And he did—he came through with the goods. We couldn't actually see the plants because they grow them from seedlings, but that was a big load off our shoulders; Bency and I had a few drinks on that one that night.' Wes arrived in time for the visit to Hillier Nurseries Jim was delighted: 'They offered us space for the container. If necessary we'd unload the container there, and Bency would then organise for the materials for each day of build-up to be put into daily lots, so trucks could transport them to us on-site.' But above all else, Jim was keen to see their plants. 'We went around with Robert Hillier and Ricky Dorlay and I took photos of all the plants. To me they're little babies; they're living things. It was winter over there, January, so they were quite small. I'm looking at them and thinking, "God, I hope they grow a lot between now and then." They told me they'll get a big burst of growth in spring and I hoped they would, as plants are still our weak point.'

Jim, Mark and Wes attended the media launch. 'That was a huge experience. Here were these Australian knockabouts in a full-blown press conference: BBC-TV and BBC Radio from all the regions, press—*Daily Telegraph* and the *Sun*—all the big magazines and people from all the well-known gardening magazines. We're just gardeners. You look around and think, "Goodness me, I never thought I'd be doing this; never in a million years." The PR company Rose Tinted was representing a nursery display and four show gardens, including the Merrill Lynch—the major sponsor's—garden, Julian Dowle's garden for the Salvation Army and *Australian Inspiration*. 'The sponsor of each garden gets up and does a five-minute presentation, introducing each garden. Then the designer does a 10-minute PowerPoint presentation, explaining all the design elements. Then they ask questions. Everyone welcomed us and they were really interested. I wouldn't say we stole the show, but we certainly realised there was a big novelty factor in having an Australian garden. We found that the people from the other gardens, even during their presentations, were making comments about having Australians at this year's show. Then everyone wanted to have a beer with us. There was a really good family feeling. But then it starts hitting home how big this thing is. You'd never get that calibre of media interest in Australia. You are now the focus of attention. You're a Chelsea show garden now. You've been accepted. Your site's been allocated. You're locked in.'

Following the media launch, on their last day in London, Mark and Jim met with Anita Collins, the Chelsea event director. 'Bency had dealt with Anita many times, by email and on the phone, so it was great for him to meet her in person. She was very warm and friendly. Bency had a lot of questions to ask. He wanted to know if we could get the container on-site. If our stuff had to be stored at Hillier, sorted into daily lots and delivered each day to Chelsea it would be difficult and expensive. At Chelsea, deliveries can take hours to actually get from the gate to your site, because it's just so busy. If we could get the container on-site it was going to be easy. We'd just take out the stuff as we need it; and we'd also have an instant site shed. That was going to be a big win for us. Anita was very good about it. She said it was certainly possible. She'd check the itinerary, see what other things were happening around our site, see if we could get the big truck in at that time and place the container without it obstructing anyone else.'

Jim and Mark had one more task to complete in London. They had to ascertain the exact position of the subterranean concrete structure that ran through their site. Jim was adamant, 'We wanted to find this bloody ring beam! It was too much of a risk to assume it was where they said it was, 25cm down, so we went to a hardware shop and bought a cheap hammer, a tape measure and a 70cm-long steel rod, which we nicknamed "Rodney". We got a cab down to the Royal Chelsea Hospital on a grey, cold, drizzly day. We found the open area where our site was somewhere located: the size of two open soccer fields with a stone obelisk in the middle.' Using the tape measure they located their site, marked the four corners and took some photographs. 'It was bare; just grass. We got out the plan and worked out exactly—from what Anita had told us—where this ring beam should be. We got out the rod and the hammer and—tap-tap-tap—nothing. Moved it 10cm—tap-tap-tap—nothing.' An elderly woman out walking her dog would have seen these two men through the gathering dusk, out in the middle of this mist-shrouded open field, tapping a rod into the ground. Perhaps she thought they were detectives from Scotland Yard, probing for a body! Then it happened: 'Within about 40cm of where we assumed it would be—tap-tap-tap—bang, bang, clunk—got it! We'd bloody-well found it. Bency put his finger on the rod in the ground and pulled it out. I got the tape measure and pulled out the tape: 38cm! You beauty! It was deeper. We needed 266mm, and we had 380mm.' They now knew their excavation would not touch the ring beam. 'It was the last thing we had to do on this trip. It was the last element of risk we had to eliminate. We were just so relieved. It was raining by then and our faces were red with the cold. Near our site was this wrought-iron fence and garden bed, and we buried Rodney there.' If the elderly dog-walker had seen this, she might have called Scotland Yard herself. 'We went back to the hotel, then took a cab to the airport.'

Soon after they arrived back in Melbourne the problem of the container was solved. 'We were going to have one 40-foot container. Anita told us you can't get any trucks into the grounds over 16 metres long; our truck would have been 16.4 metres. Bency and I discussed doing it with two 20 foot containers, which is what we did. The only remaining problem was that we needed to get the containers onto our site by the Friday, so we could begin work on the Saturday. But Anita told us there was going to be a large crane working near our site on the Friday and our trucks wouldn't get through. So we had to negotiate with the truck drivers to work on Saturday, their day off. We were allowed to bring both containers in, unload one and get rid of it, and then keep the other one there for a week or so.'

Now Jim knew roughly what plants they had and exactly where everything was on the site, he could complete all the plans—hopefully for the last time. 'There are 27 plans all up: detail plans, different aspects of the construction, the exact location of the firewood walls and the rammed earth walls, elevations of all the firewood. We had to know exactly how many cubic metres of firewood we were going to need.' The materials began arriving at Semken Landscaping's yard in Molan Street in Ringwood. 'CSR were supplying the Hebel blocks for around the perimeter and Sherlock were bringing in the wheelbarrows and all the other tools.' They held weekend working bees where members of the families pitched in, helping to paint the pre-cut timber for the arbours and the other structures, because they didn't want to be painting at Chelsea in the rain. The guy who supplied the pebbles, he drove all the way to Mansfield to pick them up. He screened them through a series of meshes, then bagged the sizes separately and put them into a bigger bag. All the material donated by Daisy's landscape supplies was delivered and Daisy's loaned us a forklift to help load the containers. Then the stone for the water features came in from the stone-yard.

'Peter Day from Semken Landscaping was building the water features and he's done an amazing job. I told Pete to build them like a best-in-the-show water feature. Bency said to me, "Pete's gone all out on the water features, he's almost gone a bit too all out." If Pete had built them so that all the water came out of the top only, as you got down to the larger stones, the amount of water would appear to diminish in comparison with the increasing surface area of the stones. But he's calibrated them and worked it out so the water outlets on each piece of stone are getting progressively bigger as you go down, so there appears to be an even flow of water cascading down the whole pyramid. That's pretty hard to do. He's built the most beautiful water features.'

Quantifying the amount of firewood they needed was a real problem. Jim knew they needed 55 square metres of face and around 16 cubic metres in volume; but how to estimate how much to load, short of actually building the walls to size? If they did not have enough, where would they obtain additional eucalypt logs in London? And if they took too much, what were they going to do with half a tonne of spare firewood? 'Bency came up with the way around it; the stonemasons stacked it in as though they were building the walls.' An ABC-TV camera crew came out to film the containers being loaded, for *Gardening Australia*, and Melissa King would later fly to London to cover the event for the program.

The two containers left Semken Landscaping's yard on Monday, March 1. Jim went down to the docks to see them loaded onto the *Contship Rome*: 'She left on Thursday, March 4 with our containers somewhere on the deck. We had all the plans laminated, three sets in all. One set I'd take to London and one set Marty would take. We'd placed one set in one of the containers, so if our copies are lost on the plane, or whatever, there would still be a set in the container.' If the containers were washed overboard and finished up on the beach of a tropical island, the local people who opened them would find all the materials and instructions necessary to build themselves a beautiful, hopefully prize-winning garden—simply add plants! Bon voyage, *Australian Inspiration*. Next stop Tilbury.

chapter ten

A moment frozen in time

IMAGINE A MILD autumn afternoon in 1946 in a small garden, somewhere at the edge of an outer Melbourne suburb; a place where town meets country. This is a nurseryman's garden, packed with healthy flowering plants, verdant with foliage and overhung by beautiful trees. A small lawn area has been given over to the essential war work of growing vegetables; for the cruel hostilities that marked the interminable years of World War II ceased barely six months ago. A 1936 Chevrolet utility truck stands in the self-built garage, the timberwork recently stained and still carrying the acrid smell of creosote. The ute has been newly ducoed and freshly sign-written. Its rear-mounted charcoal burner, forced on the nursery-man by wartime petrol rationing, has been removed and new paint has covered the unsightly smoke stains. The back of the ute is loaded with potted plants—several fine specimens of hydrangeas among them.

It rained half an hour ago, a short sharp shower that sent water cascading down the garage's new corrugated iron roof, and into the old wine barrel the nurseryman has installed beside the potting shed. Australia is a dry land, and the nurseryman knows to conserve water. Perhaps a round corrugated iron tank would have been more efficient, but the nurseryman found the old barrel somewhere. Maybe it serves as a subconscious tribute to his pioneering English forebears, for this garden is very English. The plants and trees are all exotic and mainly English; the Australian bush is still a forbidding place, to be kept at bay, an enemy to farmer and nurseryman alike. He has built his side fence, the one that separates his property from the encroaching open paddock beyond, in a traditional English criss-cross timber style. The other boundaries are more securely contained, perhaps against nosy neighbours or hopeful plant thieves; back and front are solid brick walls. Pa, for that is how his family know our nurseryman, fancies himself as a bricklayer. The 'old country' echoes strongly in the pattern of the brickwork, although the water-polished pebbles he has pushed into one of the mortar courses look distinctly home-grown. Had he lived by the sea, shells would have done just as well. The other side wall is typically Australian, built in a pyramid dry-stone style, using the honey-combed volcanic rock that still litters the plains west of Melbourne.

The potting shed is empty, but we see where Pa has been working, perhaps only five minutes before. There is a heap of potting mix on the slab bench, a few terracotta pots are partly filled and a number of plants stand ready to be thumbed in, perhaps to complete this last order for the day, as listed on the chalkboard on the wall. Pa was watering his vegetables when the rain arrived and he hurried under shelter without properly turning off the tap, for precious water still runs from the hose. The short gravelled driveway, leading to the cattle grid that marks the front entrance to the property, is pock-marked with puddles, and water still runs down the open drain beneath the grid. Pa will return in a moment to complete his order, back out his ute and make his last delivery for the day. He will remember to turn off that damned tap—tightly—before he goes. The ute, his pride and joy, will be spattered with mud by the time he returns, so he will have to wash it before turning in for the night.

Jim Fogarty devised the *Pa's Shed* project as a tribute to pioneer nurseryman W.R. 'Bill' Warner. 'Warner's did the plants for the Sydney show garden, which was really pretty generous of them, because Sydney is not really their market. They drove their truck up and everything, and I thought it was pretty good of them to back us up and help us out.' Some time after that, towards the end of October 2003, Mike Warner 'sort of sheepishly' told Jim they wanted to celebrate Warner's 90th year with a garden at the 2004 Melbourne International Flower and Garden Show. They wanted to do something special. Mike asked Jim if he'd like to throw his hand over a bit of paper and point them in the right direction; there was no suggestion that they expected Jim to design a garden for them. Jim immediately rang Martin Semken and told him of Mike Warner's request, 'But I'm thinking that maybe we could do a bit more than that. Straight out, Marty said, "Yep. We're in. Let's do it. Three-way joint venture. Let's do a show garden." So I rang Mike and set up a meeting for Martin, Mike and myself, for the following week.'

Not that Jim was exactly searching for an idea for the 2004

Melbourne International Flower and Garden Show. As part of their initial reconnaissance to England in May 2003, researching the Chelsea Flower Show, they had visited Lavenham, in Suffolk. Jim fell in love with one particular garden: brick walls, an old wine cask catching rainwater off the slate roof, hydrangeas and a white-washed cottage. It was quite modest, charmingly domestic and typically English. 'I had this Lavenham garden as a concept. I'd got it all drawn up. That was what we were going to do at Melbourne for 2004: an English garden at Melbourne to promote the idea of us doing an Australian garden at Chelsea.' But for Jim, the idea of designing a garden celebrating the history of an old Melbourne family nursery was very inviting. As was the idea of trying out much that he had learned from Chelsea and applying it to a very Australian theme.

W.R. Warner founded his nursery in the Melbourne suburb of Auburn in 1914. The Victorian railway boom of the 1890s had opened up this land to middle-class villa housing, and by 1914 the area was established as a 'model' garden suburb, with perhaps a smattering of market gardens and plant nurseries. The end of World War I in 1918 led to another burst of speculative suburban development, and a rash of domestic garden building inevitably followed. Warner's moved to nearby Camberwell and then in 1938 to a large property on Warrigal Road, Burwood, just staying ahead of the brick rash of constant suburban development. More than 60 years later they had settled at Narre Warren North, on the edge of the Dandenong Ranges, home to so many of Victoria's plant nurseries. Where the garden Jim was to call *Pa's Shed* fits into this history is left to the imagination. *Pa's Shed* is a show garden, not an historical diorama. It takes a moment in the life of an old nurseryman, whom we never see, and encapsulates it; frozen for a few days in the condition all show garden designers and builders aspire to—that moment when nature is completely under human control. Entering into the spirit of such a moment, spectators could expect to see Pa emerge from his potting shed, determined to turn off that running hose. Children might even expect to see Peter Rabbit, in his little blue jacket, hopping among the cabbages.

The Lavenham ideas Jim had been brooding over were certainly not wasted. Many of the small details that were lodged in Jim's subconscious from his English experiences floated to the surface and were applied. 'All these gardens we'd been through—real gardens in England—I noticed little things. Like the pattern of the brickwork at Kew Gardens. Little details of paving and how they plant in England, and the stonework and the gutters and how they recycle water off the roof. That's very English. You see that in almost every garden over there. Being at Chelsea last year and spending time with Julian Dowle, and seeing his garden and photos of his other gardens—all this knowledge and stuff I'd learned really poured out of me in *Pa's Shed*.' Jim drew the concept for the Warner's garden in a couple of hours. 'I just sat down one Sunday night in the office, some music going, no one annoying me, and I got something on paper. I put some colour into it to take to the meeting and Mike Warner loved it. I knew Marty and Bency would get it all too, because they were with me on those trips. I knew they would immediately understand about the water features: the cattle grid and the running hose. They could picture everything I'd drawn or could describe to them.'

Jim believed he had come a long way in the previous 12 months. 'To me, *Pa's Shed* was far superior to what we did at Melbourne the previous year. *Pa's Shed* was up with the big boys. I believe it would hold up well at Chelsea.' Jim had wanted to do a Chelsea garden at

Melbourne, and in a strange way this looked like being the one. 'I spoke to Marty and Bency about that the previous year. If we did a Chelsea-style garden at Melbourne we might suffer for it. People might not get it. It was going to be a risk. They agreed. They said, "You can't worry about that. Let's keep aiming high and learning more and just going with it."' Perhaps one point of departure for this garden, beyond what had been attempted at Melbourne before, was that it inspired a story, or better still, a myriad of stories; a different story for everyone who looked at it. Everyone could relate to it: their own grandfather could well have had a garden and a shed just like Pa's. It wasn't just a display garden, suggesting ideas people might like to try at home, nor was it simply a 'theme' garden. It did not promote a product in literal terms. Warner's have achieved wide exposure through this garden, but it has promoted their name and their tradition, rather than their specific plant products. It created a mood, more than an image. 'Looking back, we always knew it was going to be controversial, and it does seem to have created some debate.'

'From October I started detailing the design of *Pa's Shed*. I did the next trip over to London in November, then had the Christmas break, and that gave me lot of brain time to think about all the little details.' The original concept featured the front of a brick cottage. 'But I was always concerned that it would be too much work to build it in nine days. You need to build it, not just in elevation, but with depth as well, in three dimensions, otherwise it's going to look fake. So I was quite happy to axe the cottage.' But without the cottage, 'I did have a hole. The rear of the site, from the potting shed to the back right corner—I didn't have anything for it. I wanted to block out the site behind as well, so I went with a brick wall, using the old brick pattern I'd seen at Kew Gardens. I tried to get the brickie to not lay the bricks too well. I wanted it to look like Pa had laid the bricks himself; they were a little out of whack, a little rustic. I wanted every little thing in that garden to tell a part of the story. I wanted a back gate. I had a path, so the path had to go somewhere; it had to make sense. I ended up with a corner circle arch wall, with a back gate, then steps down to the back of the site. That meant from the front you couldn't see right through.' Even outside the site, Jim wanted to continue the story. With a curving wall, 'normally you cut brick wedges and it all looks dapper, but I didn't want that. I wanted it to look like Pa had just bogged in the holes with pebbles. Why not? Fills the gap and it's cheap; shows a bit of character and personality.'

Jim consulted with stonemasons Brad Peeters and Mark Stammers about the stone wall, even at the design stage. It was suggested they should use Colac rock. 'It's a volcanic rock, a field rock, somewhere between scoria and granite. Marty and Bency went down to Warrnambool on a job and saw these old walls. I'd bought a book on the old methods of dry-stone walling, so I read that up over Christmas. Mark Stammers and Brad Peeters built a couple of metres of it out at Daisy's and it was exactly what I wanted. Pyramid-shaped, giving it strength, with the coping-stones along the top, on edge. All true to the old methods of dry-stone walling.' In colonial times out in the Western District, the pioneering farmers and graziers had cleared these loose honeycombed rocks off their paddocks so they could graze sheep and cattle. They stacked the rocks up along the boundaries of their paddocks, building walls and fences without using mortar: true dry-stone walling. Thus the Colac rock decided the colour of the brick walls. 'I matched it with an antique brick. We used a similar brick in the Sydney show garden. It was a CSR–PGH brick—Antique Greenway. The colour was almost identical to the Colac rock.'

The material for the buildings—the garage and potting shed—also came from Daisy's. 'They had these "jarrah giants", as they called them, and these AAA railway sleepers. The "AAA" is a quality grading, so these are the best available.' These timbers are quite expensive, 'So the garage and potting shed had to be made so they could be dismantled and taken back to Daisy's, to cut costs. This proved a challenge, designing the construction. We used creosoted 4x2 uprights and the sleepers then slid down into that, so at the end of the show it could all be dismantled and taken back.' The creosoted timber made a big impact, mainly because you could smell it three show gardens away! 'I always wanted the creosote, but I was a bit worried as to how the smell would go down. I creosoted some timber down at our place at Flinders, and I thought it looked fantastic. It's got an Australian, natural, bushy look. When we started using it at the Melbourne show there were a few complaints about the odour. A couple of Warner's guys rang in sick the next day from painting with it. People were saying, "Oh, that stinks! Are you sure you know what you're doing here?" But I believe you've got to stick with your gut feeling, and if it's part of the design of the garden, then you've got to stick with that. Right down to the floor in the garage. We were trying to make the floor look real, so it didn't look like we'd just laid it. I wanted it to look as chunky and as solid as a garage floor would be. We built it with sleepers and we offset them, so you wouldn't pick up any straight lines. We used antique bricks to fill the gaps; it worked very well.

'Glenn McGrath from Light on Landscape did the lighting for us again, which was quite generous, because he probably won't get any direct work from it. He's not really showing off any product or modern technology. But the real talent he demonstrated was the ability to adapt to a totally different brief, to install lighting as it would have been back then. I didn't want any visible modern fittings. I threw at him, "Can you get me old fuse boxes and light switches?" Sure enough he got all the old gear and came in. He put in an old fuse box. We had a bare light globe hanging in the garage. They wouldn't have had a light shade. Same in the potting shed, we had another bare globe mounted up. All the cabling was externally chased, so none of it was hidden, because back then it would all have just been clamped onto the timber. He even got the old copper saddles. Glenn invested time and money in something he probably won't get a direct return from.'

When Mike Warner first floated the idea of a show garden to mark Warner's 90th year, Jim went out to their nursery in Narre Warren North. 'I saw the old car in one of their back sheds and said to Mike, "Gee, we could use the old ute." Mike said, "If you want to. We can get it all signwritten." We didn't get it re-ducoed, that's how it was. We had a meeting with the signwriter so I was able to brief him about what I was trying to achieve.' Jim had taken a number of photographs of old signs in several English villages they had visited, 'I had a pretty clear idea of what I wanted.' They began with the signage for the ute: 'Warner's Nurseries' painted in white in a classical Roman letter with serifs, arcing across both cab doors and the rear tailgate, with a black drop shadow for emphasis and 'Established 1914' in a sans serif underneath. Freehand red swirls and swashes decorated the work in a distinctly traditional style.

Jim always knew the water features for *Pa's Shed* were going to be quite different to what you would normally see in a show garden. 'Because it was a replication of a real garden, and a working garden at that, this gave us a chance to play with water in a different way, perhaps for the first time at Melbourne. So the running tap and the hose were always going to be there. That's how they irrigated back then. The downpipe off the roof with the old wine barrel, that had to happen too. That was something we'd noticed in England in all the old gardens. I think they put manure in the water and it became a liquid fertiliser and they'd fill up their watering cans and water the plants with it. I also wanted the driveway to be potholed, with meadow grass down the middle; I wanted it to look real, like it had been driven on for years. We had to have a cattle grid out the front because that's very Australian. I took poetic licence there, because I don't think they had cattle grids in the suburbs. So if we were going to have a cattle grid, let's have some water running beneath it. The broken pipes at each end of the grid were something that happened on-site. I said to Bency, "Is there any chance of getting those old glazed terracotta pipes with the big chunky ends?" He couldn't find any, but he did organise these two unglazed terracotta pipes. They were perfect, but they were new, so Brad and I broke the ends of them. Then we decided to leave the broken terracotta pieces there in the drain. So they were still there with the pebbles.' Perhaps a large truck had come in the week before and smashed the pipes as it crossed the cattle grid; the grid had even been bent to prove it. 'We were never sure if the potholes were going to work. It's hard to repli-cate something so it looks totally uncontrived. A pothole is some-thing that just exists, driven by weather and rain and traffic.' They used pond-liner in the potholes and it worked well. 'We didn't want the driveway to look new, so every now and then we placed larger river pebbles in the gravel so it looked worn down, with some of the larger rock exposed underneath.'

Much of the planting in the *Pa's Shed* garden happened on-site, without detailed pre-planning. Jim reckons that you can only plan the planting to a certain extent. 'Come the day that all the plants arrive, it's really what's going to look the best; what looks right. You can't plan it on paper. While the trees were in their positions, and the hedging, and the majority of the plants were where they were going to be, I really did the planting off the cuff.' Jim had learned much over the preceding months and believed he could at last apply what he had garnered from Julian Dowle, from Koji Ninomiya and from Chelsea. 'On the moment, off the cuff, I believe I ended up doing a better planting job than ever before. The plants kept their integrity as real plants. I was trying to create a natural, informal, non-contrived garden. This is a nurseryman's garden. This is a garden that Pa has developed over maybe 15 years. It's evolved. It's more of a "speci" planting scheme, where he's got specimen plants.'

The hard construction had been finished. 'Brad Peeters was on his hands and knees in the garden. While this garden was very designed and thought out, I did a few things that were the opposite of what you would normally do. I had flax each side of the garden seat, the culmination of the vista that ran across the site, from the meadow to the pergola and the garden seat. I remember thinking that that's too well thought out. So I got rid of one of the flax plants. I tried not to over-design the planting; so I changed things like that as we went. Brad was right up to that. He loved doing the opposite of normal. I was yelling out to Mike Warner, "We need six more of these." I was constantly thinking 10 minutes ahead of Brad, then I'd place them and Brad would plant them. I was trying to "spot" for Brad, to make sure the plants looked real, asking him to tilt the plants around the edge to create more of a spherical look, not just an upright look. We were constantly aware that we were replicating a "real" garden, so we were always aware of where the sun is, where north is, that you're presenting the plants to the sun, which is what gardens do.'

Construction was complete and planting was in its last stages when Martin Semken arrived. He had been away in Dubai for several months setting up the company International Landscape Solutions. The garden was virtually finished, but Jim had one more touch to add. 'I said to Marty, "Let's paint mud on the cattle grid from the car tyres." There was a wheelbarrow full of site rubbish, which had dirt in it. I put the dirt in a bucket, got a guy to fill it from a hose and we had a bucket of mud. Then Marty and I dipped our hands in the mud and we wiped mud onto the cattle grid. At this time, with construction finished, we had what we call a clean site, and you only allow one or two guys in there. In this case it was Brad Peeters, with clean boots or even no boots. I'm out, Marty's out, Bency's out, only Brad's in there. So I got Brad, using his hands, to paint mud on the garage floor in behind the car tyres.' Then he painted the tyres as well. The last touch.

Everyone associated with *Pa's Shed* expected it to win a gold medal at MIFGS, but this was not to be. The judges thought otherwise and awarded it silver. 'I think *Pa's Shed* will be remembered maybe as the garden that changed the face of the Melbourne show. Don Burke says it's years ahead of the others. As the designer, that's not for me to say, but I believe we brought a lot of knowledge back from Chelsea. It's a garden show; that was one important thing we realised at Chelsea. It's called the Chelsea Flower Show, and their gardens are based around the plants. Some gardens over there are about 80 per cent soft landscaping and 20 per cent hard. They went through this phase over there, about five or six years ago, where it all got a bit modern and meaningless. There was a big backlash and they've now moved forward into plant-based show gardens. That really struck a chord with us, which is why we did what we did with *Pa's Shed*. I think it's created a bit of debate. The show should be primarily about plants. That's why I hid the potting shed with plants. Some people thought I was wrong doing that. If that garden's wrong though, then Chelsea's wrong. But you can't help having your doubts. I was pretty upset for the boys, especially Brad Peeters and Mark Stammers; I think they were quite hurt, and that upsets me. You can't help but feel that you've let them down. But I think the Melbourne International Flower and Garden Show probably needed *Pa's Shed*, and maybe it will take a few years for people to realise why.'

Jim believes *Pa's Shed* illustrates the point that his experience and ability as a designer has advanced markedly since he first designed the gold-medal winner on which *Australian Inspiration* was based. 'In many ways *Pa's Shed* is a more advanced design, which is a little disconcerting. Having said that, you can't compare the two gardens. The *Australian Inspiration* garden has an integrity to it; it's a one-off garden, with the firewood walls and rammed earth walls; it's got its own character.' But Jim knows that the stress he placed on planting in *Pa's Shed* would be carried through to *Australian Inspiration* at Chelsea. 'Certainly, we've got a lot more garden beds in the *Australian Inspiration* garden than we had in the Melbourne version in 2003. So ever since *Pa's Shed*, I've been planting and replanting the *Australian Inspiration* garden in my head. Every spare moment I'm working through the garden beds. I've got the climbers up on the timber arbour, through the reinforcing mesh, I'm thinking about the Cider Gum (*Eucalyptus gunii*); is it going to be coppiced and thick enough, or will we have to substitute that? Will the Eulalia

(*Miscanthus sinensis* "Gracillimus") be tall enough, or will I finish up not using it? When we got to Chelsea last year it was intimidating, because we were looking at these replication gardens. We'd never seen that before, because it had never been done at Melbourne. We believed we could do a garden like that, but because we hadn't done one, it bugged us. But now we've done one. So I think it was the right decision to do *Pa's Shed* before building our garden at Chelsea, because now that we've done it, it's boosted our confidence somewhat.'

Unlike most show gardens, *Pa's Shed*—at least its central core—will not disappear. Warner's are rebuilding the garage and potting shed at their nursery in Narre Warren North as a public display, and as a place to house their beloved old Chevrolet utility truck. Although Warner's are a wholesale nursery and do not deal directly with the public, Jim understands they are part of the ABC's Open Garden Scheme, so perhaps *Pa's Shed* will continue to be enjoyed by thousands of gardening enthusiasts during the years to come. 'It's always sad when at the end of a show a garden gets pulled down and you never see it again. When you've spent so much time developing and designing it, and the guys have worked so hard building it, it's kind of nice to know it's going to be rebuilt. Certainly, *Pa's Shed* was a Chelsea-style garden. But I don't know if everyone understood it.' Gold medal or no gold medal, Jim is convinced their Chelsea garden would be even better for his journey into the past with Pa.

chapter eleven

This isle, this garden, this England!

JIM FOGARTY, MARK BENCE and Jay Watson—the cameraman appointed to the team—arrived in London on Saturday, 1 May 2004. They were the advance guard of the team in the final stage of this great adventure. They met up with Bryan Sparling, the old Semken Landscaping hand who hailed from the village of Lavenham in Suffolk. Bryan had been working with Martin Semken in Dubai during the past months and was joining the Chelsea team. After leaving their luggage at the apartments Mark had rented in Notting Hill, they visited the famous street market in Portobello Road and had 'a pint' at each of three local pubs. Perhaps, as they settled down to sleep back at the apartments, they may have considered how auspicious this first day was. It was the First of May—May Day—the ancient festival of fertility and fruitfulness: what an apt day for a team of gardeners to begin the last chapter of such a great endeavour! But grim reality crashed in on them early the next morning, when they awoke to heavy rain—much of which was pouring into the bedroom occupied by Mark and Bryan. Soon after, the ceiling fell in, the room had to be evacuated and an emergency call went out to the landlord's agent.

Eager to check the progress of their plants, the team picked up a hire car that morning and headed for Kent. Within minutes of leaving London they were in the countryside, marvelling at the beauty of the landscape. The weather had improved and it was now warm and sunny. They realised once more that outside the urban areas, the whole of England is a garden: fields, hedgerows, picturesque villages and springing crops. After Melbourne, still in the grip of a prolonged drought, the land seemed startlingly green. It was the beginning of the end of spring and the winter had been cold and long, but the hawthorns were beginning to bloom in the hedges, as were the creamy-white and reddish-pink flowers of the horse chestnut trees; the white cow parsley was dusting the verges. Their first appointment, set down for late afternoon, was at The Old Walled Garden nursery out of Hadley, near Tonbridge. They had left London early so they had the whole day to explore and enjoy the countryside. Perhaps as they drove through this beautiful landscape, they may have wondered what they were doing, daring to bring a show garden to England. With the whole UK a garden, how could the thousands who visited Chelsea readily accept the artificiality of a garden show? These were just exquisite fragments of garden—built in a couple of weeks, living for perhaps another week—and 'out there' was the beautiful, majestic reality of some of the loveliest landscapes in the world. These people lived and breathed gardens, they lived *in a* garden. They were not visiting Chelsea just to see the latest whizz-bang powered lawnmowers, the newest garden lighting ideas, or this year's trend in kitsch statuary. They knew their gardens and they knew their plants. How precocious of these brash young Australians to think they could bring a garden to Britain and be taken seriously! Jim was keen to switch his head into English gardens. 'We were doing an Australian garden at Chelsea, but we still had to understand our market was English.' So they went to Sissinghurst.

Set in a wooded valley, a tall brick gatehouse tower is all that remains of Sissinghurst, once a fortified Elizabethan manor house. During the Seven Years War of 1756 to 1763 it housed 3000 French prisoners of war and they did a lot of damage. It was bought in 1930 by author Vita Sackville West and her husband Sir Harold Nicolson, who restored what was left, had a lake dug and planned its now famous gardens. These include the White Garden, where all the flowers are white and all the leaves silver. 'It's a National Trust property near Tonbridge. John Patrick, one of my teachers at Burnley College, talked about it when he lectured us on garden history. Some elements are very formal, but then there's unstructured woodland and meadows. Bency was also very keen to see it.' From there they drove to Hadlow, also not far from Tonbridge, to The Old Walled Garden, owned by John and Heather Angrave. 'They'd heard of this Australian garden coming to Chelsea, and Heather had emailed me. They were very keen.' The Angraves are specialist growers of Australian plants: shrubs and climbers. 'This was a bit of a find for us. All the Hillier stock and the Ball Colegrave stock was locked in, so anything we got from The Old Walled Garden was going to be a bonus. It's a beautiful area where they are. We drove in, along little laneways, then suddenly there's the old wall, a big brick wall. We drove along, then turned into an old world garden—a walled garden. They had a really charming, rustic, overgrown set-up: half-a-dozen igloos where they grow the plants undercover to keep them away from frost. We met Heather and her dad John—and the dogs, which were called "The Dogs". It was like a scene from an English TV show.'

John Angrave established The Old Walled Garden in 1985, and his daughter Heather joined him there in 1993. John's interest in Australia was first roused by a school geography teacher, and about 35 per cent of the plants in the nursery are Australian. The nursery is the official holder of the British National Collection of Callistemon. They import their material from tubestock nurseries in Australia, and the plants arrive in tubes, growing in a completely artificial medium such as perlite and pine bark. 'They had a lot of Australian plants, some quite rare, some we didn't know. But we knew the genus: the *Grevilleas* and *Callistemons*, the *Kunzeas* and *Melaleucas*. Some of them were one-off specimens, like the *Grevilleas*. I knew they would be great for pots. There was a Smaller Paperbark (*Melaleuca globosum*) that was in flower—a little purple ball flower—that was going to be used for a pot, and they had some great Kangaroo Paws (*Anigozanthos* sp.)—a big red one—which I knew had to go in the garden somewhere. They also had an orange kangaroo paw which had good height and was in flower, and some White Bottlebrush (*Callistemon* "White Anzac"), which looked great with the kangaroo paws. We ordered several hundred plants; I fully intended to over-order plants, knowing that I wanted to use the best of the best. If we had a couple of hundred plants left over it didn't matter, because our mission was to get it looking as good as we could.'

The next morning they were on their way to Hillier's main growing nursery at Ampfield, outside Southampton in Hampshire. The weather had turned again and it was cold and raining. 'It was a bank holiday, so Ricky Dorlay, who looks after all Hillier's Chelsea plants, kindly came into work on his day off. He's done more than 30 Chelseas for Hillier, winning consecutive gold medals, so he grows good quality stock. I got into his van and the others were in the car and we drove around to where all the plants and trees were. Hillier is a huge nursery, bigger than anything in Australia; we walked through these big igloos, massive things with thousands of plants in them. A lot of our stock had been put aside, since it was being grown on for Chelsea. The quality was great. I suppose with show gardens you want your plants to be as big as possible and really, for Chelsea, you need a year or longer; you almost need to grow over a two-year period. Time was always against us; time and distance. In a perfect world we would have had them growing longer, but Ricky did a legendary job in the time he had, getting the plants together for us. The quality of the plants was beautiful. He had them in flower and the trees were exceptional, so the plants were all under control. We sourced the very best plants we could, and I was happy with that. We finished with Hillier late in the morning and drove back to London. We didn't need to go to Ball Colegrave. We knew that they would be growing the Australian wildflowers to size—30 to 35cm—diameter and height. They grow quite quickly and I know Ball in Australia, so I knew they would be perfect. And they were.'

The following day, Tuesday, they went out to Chelsea to pick up their passes and meet with Anita Foy (formerly Anita Collins), event manager. It was raining and very cold—less than 10 degrees and there was a real chill in the air. 'We took the tube to Sloane Square and walked to the Bull Ring Gate and Anita came out with the passes so we could get in. Security's very tight. The whole area was underwater. There were ducks swimming on our site! At this stage the framework for the roof of the Great Pavilion was on the ground. There was no fabric on it, just the aluminium frame. The ground where the marquee was going was a quagmire. Some of the bigger gardens had already started, but there wasn't much going on. Jay did some filming and I think it hit Bency and I that the game was now on. It looked like it was going to be a really wet build-up—really wet. It looked like it was going to get worse once we started digging. Being London you expect rain, but you don't expect water and mud like this. I could see Bency was starting to think a little differently about things. As we walked out, past the Thames Embankment, we saw these people in black and realised they must be the New Zealanders. So we went up and exchanged greetings. They'd never been to Chelsea before. They were like ducks out of water—except they were really in the water! We developed an instant camaraderie. They were going through the same stuff that we were, and that marked the beginning of some good friendships.

'Wednesday was a down day as the rest of the crew was flying in at midday on the Thursday and we were going out to meet them. That Wednesday seemed to drag on and Bency and I were climbing the walls. We were keen to get on-site; keen for the rest of the crew to arrive, to get the containers in, to get them unloaded and get into it. For us, that whole year of preparation seemed to be weighing on our shoulders. Seeing the New Zealanders starting on the Tuesday made us pretty eager to get out the shovels and start digging. It was very tense: the lull before the storm. We just couldn't relax.'

The following day they all went out to Heathrow to welcome the rest of the team: Marty Semken, construction manager; Anne Semken, team cook and 'surrogate mother'; Paul Stammers, landscaper; Mark 'Daz' Stammers and Brad Peeters, stonemasons and landscapers; David 'Charlie' Brown, labourer during the hard phase and plantsman during the soft phase. Meeting the newcomers were Jim Fogarty, designer; Mark Bence, logistics manager; Bryan Sparling, driver and jack-of-all-trades; and Jay Watson, photographer, cinecameraman and qualified horticulturist. For Jim 'it was especially good to see Marty', who had been running International Landscape Solutions out of Dubai for some months. On Friday the whole team went to Chelsea, just to mark out the site. They weren't allowed to actually start work as the commencement days were staggered to avoid congestion, with trucks and machinery coming in and out. 'So we let the boys see the site and get a feel for it, and see some of the others that were just starting.' The site contractor had brought in a massive industrial vacuum cleaner that was sucking up all the water that was still lying across the sites. 'They got rid of a lot of it, but the ground was still very muddy. The machine Peter Dowle had organised—the mechanical digger—was standing there ready to go the next morning. Marty said a few words to everyone, which was a good beginning to the whole thing; some of the crew had started as Marty's apprentices at Semken Landscaping, so he's a sort of father figure to them. Bency and I were pretty tired. Coming off MIFGS and with all the work we'd done to get to London, we were exhausted. Marty said that although we hadn't been officially selected to represent Australia, once we started on-site, as far as everyone else was concerned we were from Australia, so we were representing Australia. He had brought an Australian flag, which he put up. The people at Semken Landscaping had sent us a stuffed toy wombat as a team mascot.' Christened 'Fat Guts', he joined in the adventure, riding on the digger, being almost buried in the soakage pit and posing for photographs all over London.

The crew had the rest of the day off and were free to wander around and see something of London. 'They just went walkabout. Anne took a few of them shopping, to help her buy a load of food. BBC Interactive, the digital TV channel, wanted to do an interview, so they picked up Marty, Bency and I outside the Bull Ring Gate in a big, chauffeur-driven Mercedes, which took us to a large private garden in Notting Hill.' It was an intensive interview, 45 minutes direct to camera, question after question, to be answered as though the garden had already been built. The following day was Saturday, their official start day. 'We got up about 5am. The sun was rising and it was hard to sleep any later; we were probably jetlagged too. Got showered, made our lunch and got downstairs to meet the others by 6.15. We all caught the bus to Notting Hill Gate station, the tube to Sloane Square and then we walked to the London Gate of the Chelsea Pensioners' Hospital, off Royal Hospital Road.'

The Royal Hospital, Chelsea, was founded by King Charles II as a retreat for old and disabled soldiers, and it is still fulfilling its original purpose as a home for the famous 'Chelsea Pensioners'. James II commissioned Sir Christopher Wren to enlarge the plans, and the new buildings, built around three courtyards and designed in an English baroque style, were opened by William and Mary in 1692. Today the hospital is home to about 400 ex-servicemen. The permanent residents—the Chelsea Pensioners—wear a distinctive uniform, unchanged since the 17th century; their coats are navy blue, and on ceremonial occasions they can be instantly recognised in their scarlet coats and tricorn hats. The Chelsea Flower Show, previously known as the Great Spring Show, was transferred from the Temple Gardens, close to the Embankment, to the outer grounds of the Royal Hospital, Chelsea, and adjoining Ranelagh Gardens in 1913. As privileged residents, the Chelsea Pensioners have free access to the show at all times. The *Australian Inspiration* team often saw them strolling about in their distinctive uniform. One old gentleman who regularly dropped by for a chat invited them all to lunch at the Hospital on one occasion. Unfortunately they had to reluctantly excuse themselves: their punishing workload and tight schedule denied them the luxury of such diversions.

The Royal Horticultural Society was founded on 7 March 1804, and thus 2004, the year of *Australian Inspiration*—the first Australian show garden at Chelsea—coincided with the society's bicentenary. The inaugural meeting of the RHS was called by John Wedgwood, son of Josiah the great potter, and held in a bookshop in Piccadilly. Among the seven men in attendance—all distinguished gardeners and horticulturists—was Sir Joseph Banks, perhaps the greatest botanist in Britain at the time, and the father of European settlement in Australia. In 1827 the RHS staged its first 'fete' and this soon became an established part of the London 'season'. The Society's extensive new garden opened at Kensington in London in 1861 and the occasion was marked by the holding of England's first flower-arrangement competition. The following year the first Great Spring Show was held at Kensington. Between 1867 and 1873 the Society decentralised, with annual provincial shows being established in Bury St Edmunds, Leicester, Manchester, Oxford, Nottingham, Birmingham and Bath. The Society's Kensington garden was vacated in 1888 and the Great Spring Show was moved to Temple Gardens. The Great Spring Show, known after 1913 as the Chelsea Flower Show—for its new site—featured an enormous temporary canvas structure called the Great Marquee, which was erected upon a forest of timber poles by an army of labourers and steam-driven cranes. This was replaced in later years by two Floral Pavilions, made of interchangeable polyester panels, providing more height and light inside, as well as doing away with many of the poles. The two pavilions were again joined together in 2004, restoring the spacious single display area, now known as the Great Pavilion. Since its beginnings in 1913, an integral part of the Chelsea Flower Show has been the construction of show gardens—to demonstrate the skills and ingenuity of garden designers and landscapers—both from Britain and from countries around the world.

Just getting the crew from Notting Hill to the Chelsea show and back again was a major operation. Jim remembers the logistics, 'Bency had to get everyone weekly travel cards so they could use the bus and the tube to get to the show, and the RHS passes so they could get in. There were three different groups using travel cards, and because we'd arrived at different times, our travel cards expired on different days: Tuesday, Thursday and Saturday. We must have been quite a sight on the tube, especially during those early days when it was very wet: a bunch of Aussies with muddy boots and trousers, tired out, hair all over the place. We had enough signage on our uniforms for people to realise we had something to do with the Chelsea Flower Show. And when the show was on people knew us from the BBC coverage, so you'd get people recognising you and talking to you: we were celebrities, in a funny sort of way.'

Work began on the Saturday and the first job was the excavation. 'Peter Dowle had one of his boys driving the machine; we weren't allowed to drive it because of health and safety regulations. We dug out the sunken garden and holes for the trees; digging down to that ring beam we discovered a 60mm-diameter water main running along the top of it. We were playing with centimetres here, and that main gave us a fright, but luckily it wasn't a major problem.' It was still raining, on and off. 'Because of the sunken garden we decided to prepare for the worst. If the rain kept going it was going to finish up as a swimming pool. So we decided to dig a hole, a sump—a metre by a metre and a metre-and-a-half deep—which we filled with broken bits of concrete and bricks and rubble and gravel and sand and stuff. So if it did bucket with rain, the water had somewhere to drain to.' If the rain kept going, 'Bency would have put in a flexible pipe from the soakage pit to a pump at the back of the site pump out the water.'

The containers arrived that day, Saturday. The first one contained the firewood and the Hebel blocks; the second had all the tools. As it turned out, the only thing they forgot to pack was a pair of secateurs, that most frequently used of gardener's tools. A trip to a hardware store remedied that deficiency. 'Bency was always worried about getting the trucks with the containers in through the Bull Ring Gate, because of the combined length of each container and the prime mover. That's why we finished up with two 20-footers, rather than one 40-footer. They were pretty tight for width, but they got through the gates. When you bring a truck in there's a whole safety process. Every 50 metres there's a safety officer, so as trucks move through the show you've got people looking out for anyone walking around, constantly calling out, "Mind your back! Mind your back!" It drives you insane after a while. The excavation went well and we got the soakage pit dug and filled with rubble. The rammed earth walls were coming in on the Monday, so we had to have the footings for them finished by the end of Sunday.

'The weather was clearing by Sunday, but the ground was still very boggy. There was no grass left by now—it was just mud and water, and the soil seemed different; although it was very muddy, it didn't really stick to your boots. In Melbourne, if you get mud on your boots you could finish up with 20 kilos of clay stuck there. So once we started cutting with the excavator it seemed to get rid of the worst of the mud, exposing the subsoil, which was reasonably dry. We talked about excavating the whole site to get rid of the mud. But we didn't; we moved on. At Chelsea, all the excavated soil gets stockpiled in the Ranelagh Gardens. A lot of gardens are dug out—excavated—so they have a lot of soil; we probably dug out about 15 cubic metres. At the end of the show the soil is all brought back, the holes and excavations are filled in and levelled off and grass is replanted.

'On Sunday we concentrated on getting in the footings for the rammed earth walls, and thinking about the perimeters, the posts for the Mini Orb fence and the uprights for the shed area. Bency was keen to get the shed built so we could get the tools out of the container.' The containers had to be placed on the steel deck between the site and road; there was nowhere else they could go. 'In Melbourne you've got a fair amount of space around your site for your tools and deliveries. At Chelsea you've got no space at all.' There are neighbours on one side and behind. Along the other side is a laneway and in front is a road, both of which have to be kept clear.

'On Monday the rammed earth walls went in. They arrived first thing from Northampton on a low-loader. They arrived all intact and they looked great. I was really happy with the colour; arguably a better colour than we had in Melbourne. Rick Lindsay arrived with them, and Bill Swaney. Rick had flown from Melbourne to do these walls, and he was overseeing their delivery. They were lifted by a tele-lifter, a big machine on four wheels, almost like a military tank with wheels instead of tracks. It's got this big hydraulic hoist arm with fork tines on the end; the arm extends about 12 metres and can lift a heavy weight. We used two slings.' Rick had built a U-shaped steel structure into each section of wall as part of the reinforcing. This emerged from the top of the wall and was threaded. He had also built a steel jib that could be bolted to the steel structure on each wall section, and using the slings, the tele-lifter could lift the sections and place them in position onto the footings Paul had made. Each section had been designed to fit, down to the last millimetre, and Ricky had written the measurements in Texta on top of each section. We were then able to call in each section, off the plan, as we needed it and we just sat the walls, as separate panels, in situ, as per the plan. And the rammed earth walls went in beautifully, no problems at all. For me, the first few days were easy, because as well as the master plans, of which there were seven, we had 20 construction drawings on A3, laminated so we could use them on-site.'

By this stage Clive 'Toodie' Faiers—Bryan Sparling's cousin who was a chippie—had already begun his carpentry work. 'The pergola and the arbour were the first things he worked on, pre-cutting all the timber off to the side of the site. The timber had been pre-painted back in Australia and he was making all the mitres—all the joins; Toodie's a joiner by trade. Because we didn't know Toodie, Marty, Bency and I were worried if he would be good enough; he might be difficult to work with; he might be slow. But he was a champion, a really good bloke. He fitted in well and definitely became part of the story. It was hard for him. He usually works inside a building; in a house the concrete floors and brick walls would already exist, and his job would be to do all the inside timber joinery. He'd have wall A and wall B—fixed positions to work off.

But here he was working on an open site that was just mud, with no clean floors to work on and no fixed positions to work off. I think he found it harder during those first three days than he let on. He then began doing the framework for the firewood walls and started framing up the exterior fences.

'Once the rammed earth walls were in, the boys were able to start bull-nosing the tops of them, preparing the paving areas at the base of the walls in the sunken garden and the base for the arbour walk, which was raised. Our benchmark was the gutter at the edge of the bitumen road, at a position directly opposite the centre of the garden. This was ground zero, and every level related to that. The site step-up was 413mm above ground zero; the sunken garden was stepped down to 206mm below ground zero. So the excavation had to be 206mm deep, then down again for your paver, your mortar and your crushed rock. We dug down about 350mm with our excavation cut. The boys boxed in the base of the arbour walk, because that had to be filled with about 10 cubic metres of "hardcore", which is like a road base—it's crushed rock with fines. That came in big white 'bulker bags'; you rip the bottom of the bag and the hardcore just pours into the boxed area. The first three days were strange, because with a show garden at Melbourne you can't excavate, so from Day 1 you'd be building straight up. But at Chelsea, because you can dig, the garden went down and it was only by Day 3 that it started coming back up. So by Day 2 morale was down. We were working in mud and everyone was keen to see the garden come out of the ground—but it wasn't. You're working on stuff that no one is going to see, which is always frustrating. You're boxing up for the hard-core, which no one sees. They'll never see the footings or the preparatory work for the rammed earth walls, or the soakage pit.' The long build-up period of two and-a-half weeks stretched before them, almost like a prison sentence. Everyone was glad to get back to the apartments, no matter how late it was. They called Notting Hill, 'Not In Hell', the inference being that Chelsea was 'In Hell'. 'No one complained, but you sense things. Once the rammed earth walls went in and the weather started to clear and Toodie's timber posts began going up, morale improved.' At this time the first container went out, so they had more room on the site.

The only people on the whole Chelsea site were the crews building the 21 show gardens and the smaller gardens; the people erecting the marquees and the 'shell scheme'—the little retail stands; and the people working for Sagum Events—the site contractors. 'The contractors were cleaning up the whole of the Chelsea site. They stripped all the ground under that huge marquee—the Great Pavilion—took out all the mud, and brought in hundreds of cubic metres of sand to cover it all. They pumped in hot air, attempting to dry the ground, once the marquee roof went on. They did a massive amount of work and were probably operating 24 hours a day. There was machinery everywhere: big trucks—or lorries, as they call them—big excavators and diggers. And there were health and safety officers everywhere, with megaphones, constantly calling out, "Mind your back!" The infrastructure at Chelsea was daunting. It was not like the Melbourne show. You knew this show was BIG. And it was apparent that huge amounts of money were involved in staging the show.'

The *Australian Inspiration* crew was working hard, putting in long days and this began to take its toll towards the end of the first week. 'There were some days when people were tired and there wasn't much talking. There'd be days when morale was good and there'd be laughter and banter, but there were days when no one felt like talking. You're tired, you've got a job to do and you just do it. Toodie's last job, before he left on Day 11, was to build the jarrah benches in the lounge area. We had shipped over the recycled, dressed jarrah pieces, which Peter Barnard of Timber Search had donated. Toodie built a frame, then built in the benches, on-site. He mitred all the joins and did a beautiful job, and Marty lacquered them.'

On the Friday, a week after the site was measured up, the crew arrived at 7am to find the prime mover waiting to take out the blue container. 'We were all buggered, but we knew what we were up for, because all the firewood was still in the container. It took us two-and-a-half-hours to unload the firewood. It was the worst bloody job to get first thing in the morning, at the end of the first week, when no one had any energy. There wasn't much talking, just working in a chain: firewood, firewood, firewood. It was all mouldy because it had been on the ship for so long, then on the dock, then on the wet site, so everyone was covered in mould and crap. But it was a job that had to be done. The boys then started building the firewood walls straight away: Paul, Daz and Brad, with Charlie and Bryan labouring. They got the big logs in; then the small ones were slotted in like a big jigsaw puzzle. By that second Saturday we'd got a lot done and the firewood was all in by the Saturday night.' Getting the distinctive-looking firewood walls built lifted spirits a lot. The site was beginning to look like a garden: *their* garden. 'Most of the paving was done by this stage. That weekend they were finishing the paving and the pebbling,' mortaring the Mansfield pebbles as mosaics along the arbour walk and in the sunken garden. 'It's really hard work and quite exacting; you're down on your knees, concentrating hard. It takes skill, but it's also repetitive and monotonous. The bull-nosed capping was also quite intricate, lots of corners on the rammed earth walls and all the capping had to be cut "spot on" to fit. It was a big week for Paul, Daz and Brad.'

Glenn McGrath from Light on Landscape arrived from Melbourne on the Thursday, Day 6, and began his work the following day, installing the lighting. 'It's not an easy job drilling through the rammed earth walls. But all the garden lighting had to go in before we began planting.' There were lights illuminating the water features, as well as step lighting and lighting in the lounge area, and along the garden walk.' Theoretically, the show wasn't open after sunset, which was becoming later and later as spring moved into summer. But some of the show gardens were lit, and BBC television often featured footage shot after dark. The Melbourne garden was lit so effectively that lighting was considered an important part of the Chelsea display. 'Once he'd finished the lighting Glenn became an integral team player. He took on detail painting on the timberwork and was still touching up paintwork on the last weekend. He helped carry the firewood; he was awesome—your typical Aussie worker.' Jay Watson had joined the team as photographer and cinematographer. A schoolmate of Jim's, Jay had an outstanding record as an Australian adventurer and documentary film-maker. Jay's most recent production, *Hell on Ice*, documenting a near-tragic journey he and a companion made across the Antarctic Peninsula, was screened on ABC-TV during 2004. Jay also helped with the painting, in the most difficult and awkward places. Because of the ring beam the perimeter had to be raised a little, so two rows of Hebel blocks were placed at the front and left boundaries of the site. The Hebels are aerated cement blocks, as white as chalk. 'So they had to be painted with the rammed earth paint—earth with acrylic added—so they looked like part of the rammed earth walls.' Bryan had painted them first and then Jay went around with an artist's brush and painted under the bull-nose capping, to cover the mortar. 'But the colour was too dark, so we added some white and he had to re-do it. It was painstaking work, but he did a beautiful job. Then he repainted all the Hebel blocks in this lighter colour. But when he had finished, the Box Hedge (*Buxus sempervirens*) went in and covered much of it up!'

By the Saturday, Martin and Mark were assembling the black slate water features. David 'Charlie' Brown was carrying the heavy stone pieces across the road from where they were stacked, handing them to Jim, who was taking them into the garden and across to Martin and Mark. 'Everyone was really buggered by this stage. I was lifting this piece of stone when I heard this bloody great bang! Charlie had been carrying the biggest piece of stone, the bottom piece for the larger water feature, when he tripped on something, dropped the stone and fell down. I turned around and I saw him getting up. I felt sick. This stone was almost a metre by a metre. It must have weighed 40 kilos. I was sure it had shattered. I felt sorry for Charlie because he'd hurt his knee; plus he must have thought he'd smashed the piece of stone. What he didn't know was that Bency had shipped a spare big piece,' so it could be cut up had a smaller spare been needed. But the stone was still intact. 'We did have a back-up, but Charlie didn't know that, and it must have stopped his heart for a moment.'

They were reaching the end of the 'hard' phase and the weekend was going to be the transitional time. The team was used to nine-day build-ups in Australia. 'We were on a 16-day build-up here, so we were going into unknown territory. Marty was quite worried about how the guys would handle it.' They had worked long, hard days without a break. 'Marty came up with a strategy.' He decided to break the crew down into three or four small crews and give each of them some rest time. On Saturday afternoon, Mark, Daz and Brad were free to go sightseeing, or go to the pub or whatever. Mandy Bence was flying in on Saturday to help with the planting, so she and Mark went sightseeing on Sunday afternoon. 'Three o'clock on Saturday, I took the train up to Henley, further up the Thames. Marty and I decided I needed to switch my head from the construction phase into the planting phase. Being on a muddy construction site for a week, all day and every day, it was hard to switch over. I'd had an offer from a friend to go up to South Oxfordshire, up past Henley. I took her up on her offer and she took me to see some great gardens. One was a large private garden with a big chess set of topiary Yew trees. It gave me a chance to get inspired for the planting, and I caught a train back into London and got back to the site at midday on Sunday.'

The trees had arrived on the Thursday, and by the Saturday most of the plants had arrived as well. 'We had 26 trolleys of plants, so there were bloody plants everywhere, on the ground as well as on the trolleys. The Ball Colegrave plants turned up, and the plants from The Old Walled Garden. The Red Bottlebrush (*Callistemon citrinus* "Splendens") espaliered hedge was there, in pots on the ground. We had plants coming out of our ears! Luckily a lot of the Hillier stock was on trolleys. We had to keep moving trolleys out of everyone's way. The trees went in on the Friday, on Sunday afternoon we began preparing for the actual planting, and on Monday, Charlie, Mandy and I actually began to plant. We started at the back, in the secret garden. This was difficult because it was cramped; it was such a small area. They were keen to get in and start planting; they were a bit eager and I had to slow them down a bit. I decided to come back to that area, and Charlie and I started planting the main garden, out near the water feature, and Mandy went on to watering all the plants. At this stage it was getting quite warm and all these plants had to be kept watered. This is quite hard, because apart from keeping them all moist, every plant has to be watered before it is planted in the garden, so if someone starts watering too late, we start planting things that haven't been watered, and you lose track of what has and hasn't been watered.' Too much water and they begin to drown. 'The Ball Colegrave plants hadn't been "hardened off", which means they had come out of the igloos and into the full sun, and straight out onto the steel deck or the bitumen roadway, because we had nowhere else to put them. We were trying to shift them to a shadier spot or cover them with plastic; but they started "bottoming out". So Mandy had a really key role and she did a great job, as well as continuing with planting.' Tanya Clayton also came in on the Thursday, for the last two days of planting. Tanya had worked at Gardenworld in Melbourne, where she got to know the Semken Landscaping people. She now lives in Nottingham, where she works as a gardener, and had volunteered to help on *Australian Inspiration* while staying with a girlfriend in London. 'I got her doing more and more planting with Charlie; she was good at detailing and check-pruning; bringing a fresh eye to the job.'

Martin was determined to finish the garden by that Friday, Day 14, leaving the weekend for 'tweaking'. Also, they knew the media —reporters and camera crews—would be all over the garden by that last weekend. 'Tuesday, Wednesday, Thursday and Friday were double days. We did in excess of 16-hour days on-site. You're just in there, building this bloody garden and you've got this deadline hanging over you. Everyone's got their job to do: Jay, Glenn and Bryan are painting; Charlie, Tanya, Mandy and I are planting; and Daz, Brad and Paul are acid-washing the pavers and the pebbling.

Bency was finishing some of the carpentry and Marty was slotting in wherever help was needed. We had to get the mould off the fire-wood. Anne suggested Domestos, and it worked! Anne had a crucial role throughout all this as "surrogate mother", cooking for us every night. One night we got home at 11 o'clock and Anne, as always, had dinner waiting. During those long days it was all we had to look forward to, knowing Anne would have a home-cooked meal ready for us. She had shepherd's pie one night, and we just devoured it. She did desserts every night too: apple crumble and all that sort of stuff. She'd send us off each morning with jars of anzac biscuits she'd baked (which we shared with the New Zealanders!) and chocolate cake or chocolate slice—sugar fixes to keep us all going.'

With the deadline approaching they had to think about styling the lounge area. Jim had the cushions done by an upholsterer in Ringwood and they were off-white with wide, charcoal-grey vertical stripes. 'I thought of having a table runner: a long, narrow track of cloth, so it shows off the furniture and doesn't cover the table.' Jim wanted this rectangular shape to provide a dynamic statement, so it was at right angles to the rectangular window that allowed a glimpse of the secret garden behind. 'I had a chat with Anne about having a table runner and some black dishes on the table. I didn't want the usual round dishes. I actually wanted to get something of an Asian look into it. The garden was an eclectic garden, influenced by many regions around the world, so I wanted to bring in an Asian touch. Anne went shopping, looking for stores that had that kind of stuff. She travelled around the tube network, in and out of stations, and finally she found a store in Sloane Square, the tube station nearest to the Chelsea site. I went with her one day and had a look. They had a perfect table runner. I wanted that natural colour: an off-white, beige sort of colour. We found some square, black African earthenware dishes too. We bought four small ones and a big one. I wanted some candles, which Anne also sourced, and we wanted something to go in the bowl: fruit or nuts or something. We couldn't think of anything Australian, so we settled on avocados: dark green, almost black and Australian in lifestyle.'

During those last few days the number of people moving about the Chelsea site was steadily increasing and the crew were constantly being distracted by passers-by asking questions and wanting to talk to them. Parties of students were coming through, guided by RHS people, and of course they were keen to ask questions and make comments. This interest in the garden was heartening, but it also made it difficult to work. 'I started putting earmuffs on and ignoring everyone. The planting was not something you could do off a plan; it was almost spontaneous. So I had to give it my full attention. With the earmuffs on I could block out all the distractions.' Martin was also aware his crew was suffering from a steady stream of interruptions. 'So Marty put "earmuffs" around the site, positioning plant trolleys around the perimeter and leaving a one-metre gap at the right-hand corner so we could come in and out. It worked—it stopped the distractions. He locked us all in and allowed us to get on with it.' Finally they reached that last Friday. 'It was about 9.30pm and the boys were just finishing the washing-off and the painting and the planting was done.' All that was left was the styling, placing the cushions and dressing the table; that and the final 'tweaking': trimming grass, pruning and re-shaping errant plants; even washing dust off the larger leaves. 'As far as construction and planting were concerned, the garden was finished.'

chapter twelve

Gold-plated garden

THE ASSESSORS FROM the Royal Horticultural Society visited all the show gardens during that final weekend. Jim knows that their role is to do a lot of hard work for the judges: 'They do a lot of the groundwork and then the judges are able to judge relatively quickly—and look for the "wow!" factor.' The assessors are looking to see if the gardens have reached the standards they have set out to achieve: if they have fulfilled their design briefs. 'They come around, either on their own or in pairs. You'd pick them a mile away, dressed like English gentlemen: jacket, pants, shirt, tie.' Jim believes they even recommend if a garden should receive a medal, and what medal it should be: bronze, silver, silver-gilt or gold. The judges use the information the assessors give them, consider their recommendations, but they always reach their own decisions. 'The judges came on Monday morning, about 10am. We'd arrived quite early, about 8 o'clock, but as soon as they arrived, Marty, Bency and I just wanted to disappear. And we did. You never want to be there during judging, even in Melbourne. As soon as your garden is finished, the worst thing you can do is hang around. You've got to cut the tie. You even try to start thinking about the pull-down,' anything but what the judges may be thinking or saying to each other. The judging seems to operate almost like a jury in a trial. Individual judges argue and negotiate for their favourite gardens to win gold medals, but the final result seems to come down to a system of hands-up voting. 'Even in the final judging, three or four of them might have voted gold, but it may not be enough to bring your garden over the line.'

Monday was Media Day, and once the judges had been through, the *Australian Inspiration* crew awaited the arrival of the press: journalists, photographers, camera crews and broadcasters. Media people had been wandering past all weekend. Jim, Wes, Martin and Mark had been granting one interview after another, photographers had been lining up their favourite shots and camera crews had been shooting footage, preparing for the plethora of television coverage that would follow during the week to come, especially on the BBC. These segments would be introduced by a gaggle of well-known commentators and celebrities, who would stand in the garden and pass their opinions on to millions of viewers all over Britain. Most of their comments would be positive, even congratulatory. 'We were getting great comments. One of the good things about garden shows is that you're probably not going to appeal to everyone's taste, but every show garden at Chelsea will be getting very good comments because the standard is so high.' Germaine Greer, expatriate and expert commentator on all things Australian, was interviewed by BBC-TV, standing in the garden. She remarked that it wasn't a typical Australian garden. It was 'too tidy'! However Bob Geldof went by, and in a throwaway line said, 'This would be great on my rooftop.' If you had a pass, Media Day was by far the best day to visit the show. The place was not crowded and all the gardens and floral exhibits could be viewed in comfort. As well as the press, Monday was also reserved for a number of VIPs who wore passes proclaiming them to be 'Monday Specials'. Hence the presence of Bob Geldof, Ringo Starr and a number of other celebrities. Many of those visiting the Australian garden made enthusiastic and congratulatory remarks. The Australian crew played 'Pick the Personality' all day. 'The Duke and Duchess of Kent walked past and all sorts of well-dressed English notables, and we had no idea who many of them were!

'We were beginning to realise at that stage that people were probably warming to us because of the people we are: open and friendly and welcoming. So as well as the garden drawing attention, we were attracting a lot of goodwill. But it was also a difficult time because we were so exhausted, not only as a result of the build-up, but also following the whole lead-up: flying to London, worrying about the weather and then the plants—we didn't have much left in us. Martin had gone full steam ahead during the build-up, he didn't have any time off.' But now, facing the press in a steady stream was hard work. 'We had all the British media and the Australian media that came over, and the phone interviews with Australia. That's quite taxing. You're asked endless questions. It's like doing an exam, over and over. You try to speak well, to give them all the right information, always thinking ahead of what you're saying. But it's all good fun. Suddenly the garden is finished and everyone is starting to enjoy it; it's actually quite a buzz.' Hanging over everything, however, was the reality of the following day, Tuesday, when the judges' decisions would finally be known.

Midway through Monday afternoon everyone had to leave the

show except certain nominated people from each exhibit and show garden. 'Usually, I think only garden designers and sponsors received royal passes. I don't know why we got four passes, but the RHS were generous in letting all four of us stay. Perhaps they realised we'd come a long way, had worked hard and had brought a bit of character to the show. It would have been difficult to do it without Marty and Bency, because they've been a big part of this story, going back to the beginning. Can you imagine the whole show with no one there, just the exhibitors on each garden? It was like a ghost town with deserted streets. First the bomb squad went through, then the sniffer dogs. Then all these royal cars—big black Bentleys—drove slowly past us along Northern Road. Then a security bus, empty. They'd obviously dropped all the royal party, and the security people, off at the Bull Ring Gate, then they were going through and exiting out the back of the show.' Prince Edward and Sophie were the first royals we met. I stepped forward, introduced myself, then introduced them to the others. They commented that we'd had really good weather for the build-up, but we explained how wet and cold it had been when we arrived. We told them about the ducks swimming around on our site. "What did you do with the ducks?" Prince Edward asked. "We ate them," the boys replied, indicating the barbecue. They roared with laughter. It's probably not something you should say to royals, but they knew we were joking around.

'They left and we waited and waited: it seemed like hours. Then several police arrived in their tall "bobby" helmets. They came up and stood next to us. It was a really strange, surreal feeling: you're going to meet this fantastical person. Then the protocol person came up with her clipboard and asked for me and said, "You're to receive Her Majesty, then you call her 'Ma'am' thereafter and you introduce the other members of the team, and you have a talk to her about the garden." No big deal. Soon we could see quite a throng of people up on the next show garden. Then suddenly the Queen is walking down the road on her own, ahead of her entourage, walking right up to us. I greeted her. I didn't bow or anything. Sir Richard Carew Pole, President of the Royal Horticultural Society, introduced Her Majesty to myself as the designer. I shook hands with Her Majesty and welcomed her to "a little piece of Australia at Chelsea". We had a one or two-minute chat about the garden, then I said, "I must introduce you to our sponsor, Mr Wes Fleming, our team manager Mark Bence and our construction manager Martin Semken. So we had a really relaxed conversation with her. She seemed just like a grandmother. Although she's the Queen we didn't feel intimidated. We were a little overawed, but it was all so relaxed. She loved the garden. She said it was nice to see some different plants at Chelsea. She was intrigued by the firewood wall and I made the comment that the river-washed pebbles came from a stream up near Timbertop, where Prince Charles went to school. We talked about the plants: the kangaroo paws and bottlebrushes. It was nice to just stand there and watch the Queen enjoying this garden, appreciating all the hard work everyone's put in. I wished everyone could have been there to share it—the crew in London with us and everyone back home in Melbourne.' The ducks were not mentioned.

After the royal visit came the Gala Preview, staged between 6 and 9pm, right across the entire show ground. 'They set up trestle tables with big platters of food and wine and champagne—no beer. We had beer in our shed, so we were the only people drinking beer. It was all corporate people and their guests, with the proceeds going to charity. We were told that these were very wealthy and prestigious people; someone commented that the most powerful people in Britain were gathered in that place that evening.' Everyone simply wandered about, eating and drinking and admiring the gardens. 'The response was great. We kept getting very favourable comments about our garden. We stayed with our garden for a while, then we wandered about, enjoying the entire show. The lights were on in our garden. It still wasn't dark, but it looked great. Glenn McGrath's lighting was stunning. The BBC filmed it in the dark, with all the lights on. It was something of a luxury, doing lighting. We knew the show wasn't open at night, but outdoor lighting is becoming a key component of gardens in Australia.' The garden was intended to be an outdoor room, an entertaining area, 'and we live outdoors a lot, so it was important to have lighting. Even during the day, the light fittings are a detail in the garden in their own right.' But although the Gala Night was a vastly enjoyable experience, 'We couldn't relax, because we knew the big day was beckoning, and that was Tuesday —judgement day! So we left about 9 o'clock and went home to bed, very tired—and slightly anxious.'

'On Tuesday morning we got the whole team together and we all went to Chelsea early.' In Melbourne, if you've won anything, they come around and affix a large, printed facsimile medal—bronze, silver or gold—to the sign at the front of your garden, either very early in the morning, or even overnight. So the *Australian Inspiration* team expected to know the worst—or the best—as soon as they arrived. Jim explained: 'Because Jay was going to be filming, we walked in as a group. Everyone said, "Jim, you've got to go first, because you're the designer, then we'll all walk in as a group." We were all in uniform. As soon as we turned the corner three BBC cameras pounced on us! We didn't know what that meant, whether it was good or bad.' The cameras may have been looking for a disappointing response at finding nothing, or an outburst of spontaneous joy, when a medal was discovered. 'Obviously, filming the Australians arriving in a group in their uniforms was good footage, whichever way it went. There was a camera right in my face as I walked up Northern Road towards our garden, with a couple of cameras behind, filming the rest of the group. I remember thinking that I don't know what this means, whether we've gone badly or done really well, but I was so proud to have that bunch of men and women behind me.

'We got to the garden and there was no medal on the sign. But there was a letter lying at the front of the garden. I opened it, wondering if it was going to tell us that they appreciated all our work, but they'd decided not to award us a medal. But it was just a notice telling us how to evacuate the site during a bomb scare, or where to stand during an emergency, or something. But that really put us off, because we'd had this really big build-up with the BBC cameras all over us, to discover there wasn't a medal at the garden. We didn't know if that meant we hadn't got one, or they hadn't put the medals out yet. We didn't know the routine. My first reaction was, "Shit! We've got nothing!" But at the back of my mind I was hoping they hadn't put the medals out. It was a dreadful time.

'What we didn't know was that at 7am London time the results were posted on the Internet. My mobile phone was constantly buzzing in my pocket with people trying to ring from Australia, congratulating us. But I didn't answer it. I wanted to fully enjoy the moment of finding out officially; anyway, they may have been passing on bad news. An Australian journalist came up. She had a release from the press tent and she broke the news to me. But I think she realised straight away that I didn't want to find out like that, I wanted to find out officially. Don Burke was there with his film crew. He was obviously there to film our reaction to the good news; but he saw straight away that we obviously didn't want to know. He saw this other journalist attempting to break the news and he obviously realised what an awkward moment it was for us. He got his crew together and they packed up and went away and left us in peace. He eased that moment for me. There was a lot of people around, and all I wanted to do was sit somewhere quiet and wait for the moment, because it was the culmination of a lot of things. Don interviewed me later and it went very well. I feel very grateful to Don; what I am doing now is partly because Don Burke filmed my first garden at MIFGS, eight years ago.

'Not long after we saw the RHS people with the BBC film crew at the Merrill Lynch garden, up at the corner of Main Avenue. Then they came along to our garden: a couple of girls dressed in black. We were all milling around and it was obvious they had the award for us, if there was one. They found me, and the BBC cameras were rolling, and it's such a blurred moment, I can't remember if it was in an envelope, but I read the certificate: "It's silver-gilt!" Jenny Bond, the BBC royal reporter was there, and—bang!—she asked me: "How do you feel right now?" I don't remember what I said I was so over-awed by the whole thing. I was very happy. Of course you're always after that gold; but you're trying to take it in, what does silver-gilt mean for us? Of course it was a bloody huge achievement. To get anything above a bronze medal would have been out of the world for us. I think I said something like: "Getting to Chelsea was a gold medal for us. We didn't come here expecting to win any medal, and to get silver-gilt is beyond our wildest dreams." In a nutshell, that's the truth. Then suddenly there was champagne—I don't know where that came from—and Marty popped the bottle. It was a sudden release of tension. There was dead silence for a few moments, then Marty came up and put his arm around me. I think the whole experience of the past 12 months suddenly hit us. I think it hit everyone around us. Then Bency joined in. We're not blokes who put our arms around other blokes, but it was just hitting us. Bloody hell, we've got a medal at Chelsea! It's very hard to get silver-gilt. Gold and silver-gilt are in the top echelon, and silver-gilt to gold is a very fine line. We know all that, so we had no qualms at all about winning silver-gilt.

'Then someone broke out the beer and there was a great photo of us all next day on page 3 of the *Australian*, sitting in the garden, drinking beer.' Melissa King, of the ABC-TV program *Gardening Australia* was there, with Jay Watson on camera, attempting to use this group in the garden as background to her commentary on winning the medal, but each time Jay rolled, someone stood up and walked out of shot. Take after take followed with Melissa repeating her lines, until finally she and Jay were satisfied. If the media had been hectic on Monday, the official Media Day, it was even more intense now that they had won a silver-gilt medal. 'Endless media: BBC—Charlie Dimmock from UK *Groundforce* and Alan Titchmarsh—they're big celebrities over there, they filmed us several times. The BBC had these huge boom-mounted cameras for overhead shots, as well as three or four cameras on tripods, with a dozen production staff all up. BBC Radio had roaming broadcasters with transmitters on their backs. Carol Klein, who presents the official Chelsea Flower Show DVD, did her opening segment in our garden. We had print journalists from Australia and Britain and from around the world. Italian *Vogue* interviewed me! Peter "Friar" Smullens—an Irish landscaper who had worked with Marty and Bency—and his mate Steve saw us celebrating our win on the BBC in

Ireland, so they decided to fly over and party with us. They ended up working with us for two days, helping with the pull-down. We bloody needed them, we were so exhausted. During the public days, we had people asking us to sign their show programs, and getting photos with us, because they'd seen us on TV.

Press coverage of the garden was equally impressive, both in Australia and Britain. A review by Katharine Swift in *The Times*, London, appeared on Saturday, 22 May. Entitled 'Home among the gum trees', it was informed and full of insights and is worth reprinting at some length:

> ... *It may not be a native garden, but it is certainly Australian, with its use of Australian materials and techniques, and its roots in the Australian landscape. Fogarty has taken the colours of the Outback as his inspiration: the earthy tones of natural woods such as jarrah and oiled redgum for the furniture and stepping stones across the lawn; the deep rusty brown of rammed earth—a traditional Australian technique—for the retaining walls; the weathered charcoal and ash-grey finishes, 'like after a bushfire', according to Fogarty, given to the exposed timber of the pergola and arbour, echoed in the tones of the bluestone copings for the retaining walls. Man-made reminders of the Outback are the 'Mini Orb' corrugated iron fence and the rusted steel of the containers and rear wall—a note picked up in the pavers of black iron-bearing granite from the Mornington Peninsula in Victoria. Even the extremities of the Australian climate are evoked by the Mansfield River pebbles swirling around the perimeter of the garden, contrasted with the sound of running water from two pyramid-shaped water features (also designed by Fogarty), made from slabs of natural black slate. The planting is predominantly bronze, grey-green and silver, reflecting the hot, dry conditions of the Australian landscape...*

The (firewood) wall is lovely, and is certain to spawn a thousand imitations. It is a timber version of a gabion (a metal cage filled with stones, originally used for shoring up the sides of motorway cuttings, but now found in the smartest of minimalist gardens as a design feature). But this log-pile wall, consisting of a timber framework in-filled with logs placed end-to-end, is softer in effect and altogether more fun. The round cut ends of the logs give pattern and surface texture to the wall, and smell delicious into the bargain. (A home-grown substitute would be silver birch, which has its own characteristic and lingering scent, plus alder for its deep red colour.) It is practical, too— a space-saving way of stacking wood, says Fogarty. 'Just pull out the logs if you want to, and use them on the barbecue.' ...

Interestingly, all the Australian plants have had to be found here, since quarantine restrictions forbad their importation. When I checked this out, I found that they are all surprisingly easily available. This means that they have already proved their worth in the British climate. Maybe next year all our gardens will be full of kangaroo paws and log-pile walls.

For Jim, the overwhelming interest and attention during the four public days 'was exhausting, but it was also a lot of fun. It's always great having a garden that people enjoy; seeing the faces of the public. On the public days you've got so many people around the garden: up to 10 deep. People struggling to get a look, holding their cameras up high, people wanting to talk to you; Wes, Marty, Bency and I were constantly signing autographs, having photos taken with all these people. I was amazed to find people from Australia coming up—people we didn't know, we'd never seen before. They'd followed our story and they'd flown over. That was a bit of a wow. They must be very keen gardeners.

'I think the name of the garden is appropriate: *Australian Inspiration*. I think the story of who we are, just landscapers and gardeners, and where we had finished up, did inspire a few people and it was really nice that they'd followed our story and they'd come all that way to see our garden. People must have booked months before, because Chelsea tickets sell out early. I loved standing back, watching their faces, seeing people react to the garden; watching where they take photos. From a designer's point of view, you're trying to provide them with photo opportunities, so it's interesting to see where they're taking photos. I also liked watching the people who were handing out the brochures. Some of them had worked on the garden, but some had not. The PR company organised some girls to come in to help with the brochures. They hadn't seen the garden before, but it was nice to see them also claiming ownership of the garden. They took real pride in it, just as we did.'

Perhaps the heroine of those public days was Tanya Clayton, who had joined the team as a volunteer in time for the planting. Unlike most of the crew, who took a well-earned rest during the show itself, Tanya remained on duty right through the public days, fielding questions non-stop; able to answer the most difficult questions because of her expert knowledge. She was pleasant, polite, friendly and informative. Her pride in the garden was obvious. 'I think Tanya is so typically Australian. She was a legend. And she did it all for free!

'Wes did a great job on the brochures. He organised them and he manned the garden constantly, answering questions and having a joke with everyone. Because we copped a bit of flak in Melbourne over the woodstack wall, with a few people accusing us of wilfully cutting down trees, Mark often called out, "No trees died for this wall!" Marty always came back with, "And no kangaroos died for these kangaroo paws!" That always got a good laugh. I think we distributed 30,000 brochures; and we ran out.

'There was one couple who had followed our story from Australia. Marty and I said, "Come on, come into the garden and we'll take a photo of you in the lounge area." They responded, "Oh, no, we can't do that!" They were overawed by it all. But they did come in and we took their photo. I don't think any of us, for a moment, forgot how special it was to be at Chelsea, even for the punters. It was a special moment for them to come into our garden and we never forgot that. We had some of the old Chelsea Pensioners come in and we'd get photos of them. I remember this really old war veteran—I think he fought at Tobruk and had a special spot for Australians. He came wearing his medals and full regalia. Marty took one arm and I took the other, and we walked him into the garden: "Come on, come on, we'll get a photo, no steps, no steps!" Of course there were steps everywhere, but we lifted him over them. Everyone was laughing.

'Chelsea's so powerful. Even when you arrive by tube you sense the power.' The New Zealand garden at Chelsea was part of a huge tourist promotion, riding on the success of *The Lord of the Rings* movies. Indeed, one of the garden's designers was a set designer on the films. One entire gallery at the Sloane Square tube station, the nearest to the Chelsea site, was given over to the New Zealand garden—dozens of placards lined the walls, with the slogan: 'New Zealand, now growing at Chelsea', and at the end, which everyone saw as they headed for the platforms, was a rolling display of New Zealand and Chelsea Flower Show scenes. The RHS must have really appreciated the cross promotion. Jim remembers, 'On the first open day, the whole road, from Sloane Square to London Gate, was barricaded and packed with people. And the queues! I thought, "My god, and this is just a garden show! This is huge!" You can't go there, even as an exhibitor, and not feel that rush of blood. To walk up through the middle of that happy, good-tempered crowd and get straight in with your exhibitor's pass—it's hard to believe you're part of this show; you're part of history.'

The last day of the show—the Friday—was perhaps the most enjoyable for the *Australian Inspiration* team. That morning the Australian High Commissioner, Michael L'Estrange, had invited them to Australia House for an informal reception. Wes's parents, Dawn and Don Fleming, had met the High Commissioner at an ambassadors' luncheon arranged by the RHS. In his address, RHS president Sir Richard Carew Pole said, 'I want to make particular mention of our friends from Australia. We have given you a silver-gilt medal, now I think it is only fair if you give us back the Ashes.' Michael L'Estrange replied, 'Officially, no deal!' At lunchtime on the Friday the BBC filmed a cooking segment, as part of their Chelsea coverage, in the Australian garden. Jim knew the *Australian Inspiration* barbecue couldn't be connected because of health and safety regulations, 'so the BBC brought in a portable grill on legs. They had a celebrity chef, James Martin, who is very well known in England, with Jenny Bond and Charlie Dimmock as presenters.' Jim and Tanya were invited to help with the cooking, and the rest of the team were filmed in the lounge area, drinking beer and enjoying the food. A quantity of Australian wines arrived, courtesy of the High Commissioner. 'The BBC catered for everyone. There were prawns and chicken burgers and lamb kebabs: mountains of food. They were there for hours after they'd finished filming, having a drink with us and enjoying the food. It was a really nice gesture.'

Then came the plant sell-off, 'which went for about an hour. I suppose we sold about a quarter of the plants, maybe more. Not an auction, just on-the-spot negotiating, bargaining and haggling, all in good fun. Our prices ranged from three pounds, up to fifty pounds. I suppose that's $7.50 up to $125. You might even give them one for nothing. They weren't in pots; they were put into plastic shopping bags we got from the RHS. It was funny afterwards, because you can't drive to the Chelsea Flower Show, there's no parking, so everyone's on the bus and the tube with all these plants they've bought. Everyone's walking out of the show and almost everyone's carrying at least one plant. It's such a part of the culture of the show, the sell-off. It's totally informal and unstructured and it's all so good-humoured.' English people can be staid and formal, but there are certain traditional times when they behave with a joyous spontaneity, such as the Last Night at the Proms concert: funny hats and streamers and singing *Rule Britannia*. They have more fun than you can imagine. Sell-off at the Chelsea Flower Show is another such occasion.

Julian Dowle had become a special friend of the Australian team across the many months preceding the show. Jim Fogarty regards him as his inspiration and mentor. During build-up and the show week itself, this bond grew even stronger, as Julian encouraged the Australians, offering many courtesies and kind gestures. His son Peter had operated as the team's English liasion. This year—2004— was Julian's last Chelsea. After designing 25 show gardens, 10 of which had won gold medals, Julian had announced that this was his swan song. Entitled *From Darkness to Light*, it had been built for the Salvation Army. Symbolising the Army's work in bringing people from the darkness of poverty and despair into the light of well-being, the colour palette of the planting moved from black, purple and red through to gold, silver and white. Capping the site was a stylised bandstand, reminding us of the Salvationists' proselytising through music. Many commentators thought it was the most beautiful garden in the show. Imagine everyone's surprise and dismay when the judges awarded it—not best in the show, not gold, not silver-gilt—but a silver medal. However, that Friday afternoon the BBC announced that its People's Choice Award, for which thousands of viewers and listeners had been voting all week, was going to Julian Dowle's *From Darkness Into Light*. It was the sweetest vindication anyone could ask for. As soon as Julian received the news he headed for the Australian garden to share it with his special friends. The party that began with the barbecue was still underway, and Julian's brilliant news capped off the celebration. 'He was such a part of our story, we were just so proud and happy for Julian.' And so the party continued with a lot of people just dropping in: small-garden designers, Salvation Army people, the governor of Her Majesty's Prison Leyhill (who were again exhibiting at Chelsea), the New Zealanders (their great effort had been rewarded with a gold medal), and many other exhibitors. Jim looked about and suddenly realised that his garden had realised its potential. People were sitting around on the benches and the rammed earth walls, drinking, laughing and enjoying themselves. Designed as an entertainment area, in the final hours of its existence it became just that. No longer just a show garden, it had fulfilled its destiny. 'As a garden, it was alive at last.'

'On Saturday we began the pull-down. You always know they've got to come down. It's part of show garden psychology that the gardens get pulled down. It's always a bit sad. I think the sadness comes more from the fact that the whole experience is coming to an end. It's not so much about losing the garden. That garden will never be built again, it's a one-off. A fair bit was salvaged, but as it turned out the rammed earth walls couldn't be re-used. Nor could the Hebel blocks. But the pavers were saved, as well as all the plants and the timber. A charity—Groundwork—took most of it. They build gardens for under-privileged children and other good causes. I think they were taking it to three different sites around London. They took the water features, the wheelbarrows, the tools, even the firewood. Almost nothing was wasted.

'The garden came down in two days. I was stuffed, I was buggered, we all were. Peter and Steve, the two Irish guys, were great. They were fresh and they just went for it. But I was next to useless. One day during pull-down we were having lunch in this marquee. We'd bought Cornish pasties from the food van. I looked around and everyone was stretched out, asleep. It would have been a great photo, but even Jay was asleep! By the end of Sunday the garden had been pulled down. The story was finished; the garden was gone. There was just a patch of bare earth and a small hole, waiting for the RHS contractors to come in, replace the topsoil, backfill and smooth it over. We all stood around and Marty said a few words, thanking everyone.' It didn't look much now, that patch of ground, that 10 by 12 metre site. But everyone there knew that a tiny corner of the grounds of Chelsea was holy ground. It would somehow remain a part of Australia forever.

AUSTRALIAN INSPIRATION CREDITS

ON-SITE TEAM: CHELSEA

Jim Fogarty	Designer
Mark Bence	Logistics/Team Manager
Martin Semken	Construction Manager
Wes Fleming	Nurseryman
Paul Stammers	Landscaper
Mark Stammers	Landscaper/Stonemason
Brad Peeters	Landscaper/Stonemason
David Brown	Landscaper/Plantsman
Clive Faiers	Carpenter
Jay Watson	Cameraman/Labourer
Bryan Sparling	Landscaper
Glenn McGrath	Lighting
Amanda Bence	Plantswoman
Tanya Clayton	Plantswoman
Anne Semken	Cook/Surrogate Mother

SUPPORT CREW: ENGLAND

Peter Dowle	Landscape Contractor
Julian Dowle	Advisor/Mentor
Robert Hillier	Hillier Nurseries
Ricky Dorlay	Hillier Nurseries
Stuart Lowen	Ball Colegrave
Heather Angrave	The Old Walled Garden
John Angrave	The Old Walled Garden

Peter Dowle Plants and Gardens Staff

ROYAL HORTICULTURAL SOCIETY

Bob Sweet	Director of Shows
Anita Foy	Show Manager
Becky Roberts	Assistant Shows Manager
Eric Saxon	Clerk of Horticultural Works

RHS Shows Department Staff

SUPPORT STAFF: MELBOURNE

Ian Ritchie	Fleming's Nurseries
Adrian Clancy	Arborist and product sponsor
Brent Reid	Jim Fogarty Design
Amanda Greer	Jim Fogarty Design
Andrew Triantafillou	Semken Landscaping
Dean Semken	Semken Landscaping
Shane Jones	Semken Landscaping
David Nichol	Semken Landscaping
Sandra Boucher	Semken Landscaping
Lindy Gill	Semken Landscaping
Peter Day	Semken Landscaping
Peter Henderson	Henderson Seeds
Kathy Ewart	Colour Illustration

SPONSORS

MAJOR SPONSOR

Fleming's Nurseries
Don Fleming, Dawn Fleming,
Wes Fleming, Graham Fleming

SUPPORT SPONSORS

Melbourne International Flower and Garden Show
David Baker, Chairman MIFGS Board
Greg Hooton, IMG
International Landscape Solutions
Jim Fogarty Design Pty Ltd
Semken Landscaping Pty Ltd

PRODUCT SPONSORS

Light on Landscape	Glenn McGrath, Amander Flaherty
Bio Gro	Anthony Van Schaik
Sherlock Wheelbarrows	Simon Twitt
Reece Irrigation	Mick O'Sullivan
Cast In Stone	Mick Hoban
Steel Living	Paula and Charlie Johnstone
Daisy's Garden Supplies	Neil and Margaret Mulcahy, Greg Hutchins
Matt Heritage Design	Matt Heritage
Timbersearch Australia	Peter Barnard
Statewide Tree Service	Adrian Clancy
CSR Hebel	Marketing Department